D1613828

# Houses To Go
## How To Buy A
## Good Home Cheap

**by Robert L. Williams**

**Loompanics Unlimited**
**Port Townsend, Washington**

# Houses To Go: How To Buy A Good Home Cheap

© 1997 by Robert L. Williams

**Published by:**
Loompanics Unlimited
PO Box 1197
Port Townsend, WA 98368
Loompanics Unlimited is a division of Loompanics Enterprises, Inc.
1-360-385-2230

Photographs by Robert L. Williams

**ISBN 1-55950-166-9**
**Library of Congress Card Catalog 97-74039**

# Contents

# Introduction

When my wife and I bought property in the country, our first need, we thought, was a house to grace the rolling hills. The major, and really the only, problem we faced was that we had no money. We looked at house plans and we talked to builders, and we found that the only house we could possibly afford was one that we would not have accepted even if it had been free.

We wanted a large house, preferably a two-story farm-style house, and the lowest estimate we received was over a hundred thousand dollars. And we did not have even the amount needed to make a down payment on such a residence.

"Why don't we shop around," I asked my wife, "and possibly find somebody who will give us a house?"

She thought I was joking, but I convinced her that not only was I in dead earnest but that I thought we could have ourselves a house by sundown that same day.

So we went for a drive and a picnic, and when I stopped at a combination grocery store-service station, I filled up the tank on our tiny foreign car and then went inside to complete buying the other items on my short shopping list.

"What did you buy?" my wife asked when I returned and put the bags in the car.

"Not much," I said. "In addition to gas, I bought potato chips, tomatoes, mustard, hamburger buns, and pickles."

As I climbed into the car and we started to drive away, I stopped the car and pointed to a beautiful old house across the highway.

"I almost forgot," I said. "I also bought us that house."

My wife was certain by then that I had totally lost my mind, but I assured her that, again, I was as serious as a coronary. She wanted to know how much money we'd have to borrow and how we could make the payments.

"I paid cash for the house," I told her. Then I related how I had paid for the gas and groceries and then asked the owner of the store who owned the house in the huge grove of pecan trees. The man replied that the house was his.

"Is it for sale?" I asked. He told me that it was.

"How much are you asking?"

He thought for a moment or two, then said, "That plot of land is in a prime business area, and it would be the perfect spot for a mini-mall. The lot is worth, I'd say, at least two hundred thousand dollars."

"I don't want the land," I said. "How much for the house only?"

He looked at the change in his hand. My purchases came to a total of $19.27 and I had given him a twenty. He held my seventy-three cents change toward me.

"Will you give this much for the house?" he asked.

I agreed immediately, and he dropped the change back into the drawer.

And I had bought a house — for 73¢!

But what had I bought? The man gave us the keys and invited us to go look over our purchase.

Our new house was a two-story farm-style house with a tall front porch that extended across the entire front of the house. Twenty-foot columns supported the porch roof.

Inside we found on the first floor a 20 x 20 foot living room, a parlor or den about the same size across the hallway, a formal dining room, a library or study, a huge kitchen, and a breakfast nook. There was also one bathroom on that floor.

We followed the wide stairs to the second floor where we saw two huge bedrooms, a second bath, and a closed-in deck that would provide us with two additional bedrooms if we decided we needed them. All the floors throughout the house were top-grade oak, in excellent condition. There was a fireplace in the den and another in the living room, and there were fireplaces in each of the bedrooms.

Connected to the back of the house were the servants' quarters and an upstairs apartment for the live-in maid. All told, we had 12 rooms, four fireplaces, and a total of 4,000 square feet of living space.

All for seventy-three cents!

But there was a catch, of course. The house was free but the land was not included, which meant that we had to move the house to our property. And we had to pay the mover.

When the house was delivered, we had to dig footings, pour the concrete, and build foundation walls. We had to re-plumb the house and re-wire it (although with most newer houses these are not necessary steps). And we had to do quite a bit of work in order to make the house livable.

In all, we spent about $15,000 on the house. So it was not free at all. Still, we had a completed house within a very short time — less time than it takes to build a house from the ground up — and the house was actually in better shape than it would have been if we had simply moved into the house where it stood.

And when all was done, we had a house worth about $100,000. So we saved $85,000 on the deal and in return obtained a super house.

Our house became the subject of several magazine stories. We were featured in *House Beautiful, American Legion Magazine,* and a number of others. All told, more than three dozen magazines, including *Southern Living, Money Magazine, Grit, Modern Maturity, Mother Earth News, Backwoods Home Magazine,* and many, many others featured our story in their pages.

Our house cost us about $5.33 per square foot, and this figure included a deep well, septic tank, and our furniture, all of which came out of the $15,000 total cost.

So you can conclude that we really hit it lucky on that day when I stopped at the service station-grocery store, right? Wrong. It's not just luck. What we did, you can do. All over this country right now there are thousands upon thousands of houses that the owners must sell or give away.

In fact, shortly after we moved the house one of my colleagues approached me and, only half-jokingly, told me that I was the luckiest SOB he had ever met in his life.

"I have dreamed for years of owning that house," he said. "I can't tell you how much I wanted it, but I knew I couldn't afford it."

"Why didn't you just ask for it?" I asked him. "It has stood there, vacant, for at least three years."

"What kind of idiot would go up to a house owner and just ask for the house?" he demanded. "I'd feel like a fool."

"I'll tell you what kind of idiot would do that," I said. "A very happy one who now owns the house of his dreams. And I don't feel like a fool. I feel like a king. A very wise one."

We like to feel that what we did benefited everyone. There are houses like ours all over the country, and if these houses aren't moved, they will be demolished and the debris hauled off to the landfill. Or the houses will stand vacant and become havens for hoodlums, magnets for vandalism, or nests for rats and snakes and insects. They will become eyesores that detract from the value of surrounding houses.

Can you still get houses as cheaply as we got ours? The answer is an emphatic **YES, YOU CAN!** In some cases you will pay more, but you may well get more. What you spend and what you get will depend largely upon how well you do your research and how well-prepared you are before you begin the hunt.

What sort of houses are available? How do you go about buying one and arranging to have it moved? How do you know that the house is road-worthy and fit to be moved? How do you know what amount to bid on a house? Where do you find houses that are going to be moved? What sort of financing, if needed, is available? Will insurance companies cover houses that are moved?

What can you do to make the cost of moving faster, easier, and less expensive? How do you select a mover? What are your options when it comes to moving the entire house? What if the house is too large to be moved? What are the tax advantages or disadvantages?

Can the chimneys be moved with the house? What is the value of the house, relative to houses that have never been moved, after the house is on the new lot? What sort of damages should you expect during transit?

These questions, and many, many more will be answered in the pages of this book. You will see photos of houses that will be moved, that are being moved, and that have been moved. In some cases you will be provided with the costs of moving the houses that are pictured, but you must keep in mind the fact that prices vary across the country, and from year to year, even day to day. You should also be aware of the regulations that govern house-moving from state to state or even city to city.

But, all variables notwithstanding, this book will help you to locate, select, buy, move, and set up houses that are cheaper than you could have dreamed possible. You will be told how to buy houses that are dirt cheap, how to secure others that are totally free, and, perhaps best of all, how you can make incredible sums of money by moving, restoring, and selling houses.

And now, it's time to start looking for houses to go — for a song. Good luck, and good fortune! Save the house, save tons of money, save yourself the frustration of overseeing the builder if you go the traditional route, save the environment, and above all save the beauty and excellence of these old houses that need someone to care for them.

# Chapter One
# How to Locate Houses to Move

Before you can consider moving a house, you must locate the house. Or, more accurately, you should locate a series of houses.

Lesson Number One is this: Just as you are not likely to buy the first suit or pair of shoes you see in a store, you should not buy the first house that is made available to you.

Shop around. Look at several houses. Look at dozens, if possible. Examine them from as many critical viewpoints as you can imagine. Learn to spot potential future problems and to avoid them.

When you decide to go shopping for a house to move, there are several places to look, some of them obvious, others that are somewhat unexpected. A general rule of thumb is to start looking as close as possible to the future site of the house. If you own property to the north of town, don't start house-hunting on the south side.

1. When you start your search, look first in the ad section of your local newspaper. Many times people will advertise a house that must be moved. As soon as you see the ad, move fast. Call immediately and ask for the particulars. If you are satisfied with what you learn, set up an instant appointment to see the house.

**Figure 1-1**
*An example of a house that was demolished because no one would move it.*

2. Watch for feature stories in the local newspaper or in larger area papers. Occasionally you will see an article about a house that will be given away to anyone who will pay to have it moved. This is not a particularly good way to find a house, because in many instances the house is so large or the move is so difficult or

**Figure 1-2**
*This house was moved from a highway project and saved.
It is now worth many times what it cost to move it.*

the time is so limited that you will have to pay far more than you normally would. Still, it will not hurt to check out the houses and talk with a house mover. Figure 1-1 shows a house that was offered free to anyone who would pay to have the house moved. However, the house was so large and the move would have been so difficult and expensive that it was impossible to find anyone willing to take the risk of having the whole house transported to another part of town.

3. Here is a superb place to find houses! Watch for news stories in local papers, on television, or on public notice boards that the highway department is planning to widen a road or highway, or build a new road, or re-route an existing highway or street.

When the state decides to widen the highway, the houses that previously sat a comfortable distance from the road will now be too close to the pavement. Houses with spacious front yards will suddenly have no yards at all. When you learn of the public notice, call or pay a visit to the local highway division offices and ask them about the houses which will be moved or demolished.

Drive to the scene. Look over the houses. Talk with owners about the conditions of the houses.

A word of advice: In many instances when the state in a sense forces homeowners to sell, the state will offer a fairly impressive price to the owners, who are likely to sell the house and use the money to buy a new house in another part of town or the county.

The state now owns the houses, and they often put them up for public bidding. If you have explored the possibilities, you know what the condition of the houses is. Owners may be very direct and honest with you and tell you that the roof leaks, that termite damage has been extensive, or that dry rot has weakened sills and joists.

In a highway project area you may find as many as two or three hundred houses that are going to be moved. Do your homework and be prepared to make your bids. Keep in mind that you will often be required to move the house within ninety days of the acceptance of your bid, so before you make your bid, check with a reputable house mover to see if the house can be moved practically. Figure 1-2 shows a house that was part of a highway project area, and the house had to be moved. It was common for houses like the one pictured to sell, including moving costs, for under $10,000 and at times much cheaper than that.

Figure 1-3 shows a house that cost a grand total of $2,900, which included the purchase price and cost of moving. It cost extra to add the porch and guttering.

4. As you drive through town, you will often see huge signs in the front yards of houses. These signs proclaim the site as: FUTURE HOME OF BURGER KING or the like.

Use common sense. Burger King or Mc-Donald's or Hardee's cannot possibly operate out of the old house on the lot. The house must go, one way or another. So contact the offices of the company that is planning to build on the lot, once it is vacant. Ask them about the house and make them an offer, if you like what they tell you.

5. Be alert for special municipal projects. If a new civic auditorium is to be constructed, or if a parking lot is to be built downtown, or if some massive urban renewal project is to be undertaken, drive to the site and look over the houses that are in the path of the construction. Figure 1-4 shows a house that had to be moved in order for airport expansion to occur. You can often find great deals on such houses.

6. Watch for news on the sports page or in the religion section of the paper. Tune in to television news. If the local college or university plans to build a new stadium, learn what houses, if any, are located on the land. If a church plans to build a new sanctuary, visit the site to see if a house stands where the new church will be.

7. Be morbid. Read the death notices and bequests parts of the newspaper. If you read that

an elderly person died and left her house to the church or college, investigate. It is possible that the college will use the house for faculty housing or that the church will use it for the associate pastor. But it is also possible — and far more likely in many cases — that the college will use the space for dorm space or parking lots. The church may do the same.

**Figure 1-3**
*This house cost less than $3,000 to buy and move.*

8. Watch for new zoning regulations. Often when a new zoning law is passed, there will be houses in the area that are unfit for business use. The houses are often too old, the wiring is not up to current standards, fire exits are non-existent, the plan of the house is not conducive to business use, or the floor will not accommodate the weight of the number of people expected inside the business. Find out who owns the house and what use is to be made of the house. Then, if you like the answers, make an offer.

9. Again, be morbid. Read the obituary columns. If the deceased lived alone, chances are good that the executors of the estate would welcome the chance to have the house removed so that a new and up-to-date house could be

built on the property, or that the vacant property could be more valuable commercially than it could ever be residentially.

**Figure 1-4**
*Airport runway extension makes many houses available to move.*

10. Watch for news of factory closings or expansions. Many years ago villages sprang up around the factory, and the workers lived in the village in order to be close to their work. If the mill or factory closes, many of the people will wish to relocate. In many cases the mills owned the houses and will be eager to dispose of them. Contact mill officials to learn the future of the houses.

Do not be discouraged by the idea of mill housing. Many of the houses were very well-built and with some modest remodeling could be made into highly attractive houses.

If the mill plans to expand, the results will be the same in terms of housing. Some of the houses must be removed in order to make room for the new buildings, and one of those houses could be yours.

11. Here is a fantastic source of houses. If the local power company or the federal government or anyone else with the authority to do so decides to build a dam, a lake, or an impoundment, leap into action immediately.

The beauty of such an opportunity is that there is no way the houses can remain where they are. They must be removed, one way or another. Keep in mind that a huge impoundment will cover not hundreds but thousands and thousands of acres. Entire towns or communities will be removed, and all of the houses will go to someone who is courageous enough and fast enough to latch onto them for an incredibly low price.

12. Watch for news of the opening of municipal, county, or state parks. In many cases there will be houses on the property, and you can make your bid and perhaps buy a super house cheap.

13. Drive around your neighborhood, keeping in mind that the best house to move is, in many cases, the one nearest you. House movers charge, among other ways, by the mile and by the unusual complications of the job. Obviously, it is probably easier to move a house down the block or across the street than it is to move one through the center of the shopping district.

If you see a house that has stood empty for some time in your neighborhood, check to determine who owns the house and what his plans for it are. You might ask why it wouldn't be simpler just to buy the house where it stands rather than move it, but there may be dozens of reasons not to attempt this solution.

For one thing, the immediate neighborhood, even the next-door neighbors, may be so bothersome that you will not want to live in the house at that location. If your neighbor, for want of a better example, keeps three dozen hives of bees, your backyard would be an impossible place to relax, and swarming bees in the early summer will invade your house in their search for a new home.

What if the neighbor breeds dogs, or simply has a pack of hunting dogs that bay for hours each night when a cat or an opossum crosses the yard? Or what if the neighbor's children will make Dennis the Menace appear to be a model child?

The possibilities are endless, but the bottom line is that you can make a phone call and learn what the future of the house is likely to be.

14. Search the rural areas near your property. The country is one of the best sources of houses — to go. There are many farm houses still in excellent repair and with a charm you cannot find in the city. The history of these houses is, very often, that the parents rear their children who marry and move out. Then when the parents tire of country life or die, they leave the house for the rats and other vermin. When you see a house that has stood empty for some time (you can tell by the uncut grass, the closed look, the fact that the old car is never moved, lack of mailbox, etc., that the house is neglected). You can stop at a neighbor's house or ask at the country store to learn who owns the house. Then make the phone calls.

15. Highway projects have already been mentioned, but you might want to try calling the state highway commission. There is probably an office near you, and the right people there can tell you of projects scheduled to begin soon in your area. These may not necessarily be highway projects, but could be other state efforts which will make the houses in the area dispensable.

16. Finally, although this is not a complete list but only the starting points, call realtors. They quite likely know of a house that is not going to sell, despite their efforts, and they will perhaps introduce you to the owner. You could even offer a small fee to the realtor for his cooperation, and he might assume that half a loaf is better than no bread at all.

Make your own list in addition to the one here. The adage is that gold is where you find it, and so are houses to move going to be where you find them. You may exhaust every lead in your search, and then the man who works beside you may casually mention a possible house. Talk it up. Ask your co-workers if they know of a potential house to buy and move. If you are a teacher in high school or college, ask your classes if they know of any. Ask the members of your church or civic club or fraternal group.

You can even check with demolition firms to see if they have any contracts to tear down houses in the area. Naturally, the demolition teams will be reluctant to give up their fee, but if you can learn what they will be paid and then offer them half of that amount (with the understanding that in order for the firm to earn money, they must spend money, and that if the firm can earn its profit without having to work, they will often be very happy) you may be able to buy the house before it is destroyed.

Be relentless. You can find a house to meet your needs. In each town in this country there are houses that must, should, and will be moved. One of them could be yours.

# Chapter Two
# How to Decide Which
# House to Buy

When you locate a number of houses to consider for moving, you need to make several determinations before you put any money down as payment. The first thing to check is the actual physical condition of the house.

Termite damage is one of the worst problems. When you first arrive at the house site, make a quick visual inspection of the house and its foundation walls. If the house sits on a sloped lot, check the back of the house for distance above ground. In many instances, in order to save on cement blocks for the foundation wall, the builders barely cleared the top of the soil at the highest part of the slope. Note that in Figure 2-1 and Figure 2-2 the houses, while neat and attractive, were built very close to the ground. Movers found that in both cases, though, the houses had escaped termite damage and were very sound and ready to move.

Houses like these could commonly be bought for $25 or less. I personally found more than 50 houses in one town that could be purchased for $25 on down to $5.

When you walk around the house and see that the timbers are only six inches or so above the ground level, unless the house is in Arizona or

**Figure 2-1**
*This house was built low to the ground.*

another desert area, you might as well leave at that point. Termites must have moisture in order to survive, and if they have the dampness of the soil in close proximity to the wood of the house, they are in insect heaven. The odds are great that the damage is so extensive that the house is not worth moving.

**Figure 2-2**
*...as was this one.*

**Figure 2-3**
*Although damaged by termites, this house was repairable.*

Figure 2-3 shows a house that had been badly damaged by termites, but movers were able to jack up the house and remove the faulty sills and replace them. Then the house was considered sound and, though inexpensive, valuable. It was effectively moved to a large rural lot and became a superior house for the family that bought it.

If the house appears to be in good shape, crawl under the house and, taking a flashlight, a screwdriver or pocketknife, and a carpenter's level with you, move from joist to joist. Shine the light on the sides and bottom of the joists to see if you can spot any of the tell-tale pinholes that indicate the presence of wood-eating insects. Examine the dirt under the joists for tiny mounds or scatterings of very fine sawdust that look like brown sugar. Figure 2-4 shows mounds of sawdust created by boring insects, including termites and carpenter bees.

If you don't spot any obvious damage, you are still not in the clear. Use the blade of the pocketknife or screwdriver and punch it into the bottom or sides of the joists. If the blade sinks readily into the wood, the joist has been riddled by the termites or other insects.

**Figure 2-4**
*Boring insects leave mounds of sawdust, as evidenced here.*

In Figure 2-5 note that the board pulled from the bottom of a wall in a house too close to the ground shows advanced stages of rot. The blade of the pocketknife sticks completely through the wood. The board itself was a section of sub-flooring, and you can be sure that if the subflooring is rotted, so will be the joists and other lower timbers.

Don't settle for checking only one or two joists. Examine all of them, and check at several points along the joist. Move to the sills above the foundation wall and check every two or three feet along the entire foundation wall.

I know that this examination is time-consuming, but it will not take nearly as long as the time you will need to rip out damaged joists and replace them. You will find that trying to repair extensive termite damage is not only time-consuming but extremely expensive.

If the crawl space under the house is too low for you, you will likely find that termites have gone where you cannot. The crawl space should ideally be three feet above ground level. If it is lower, you have the moisture and rot problems in addition to the termite or other insect infestation.

Now use the carpenter's level and hold it

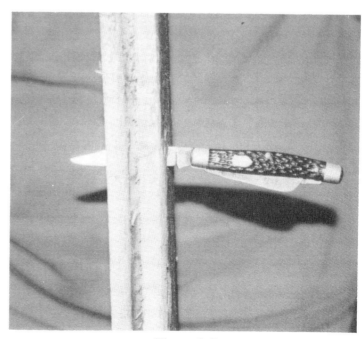

**Figure 2-5**
*Because the house was built too close to the ground, this board rotted.*

against the bottom of the joists. If you find that the joists are badly bowed, you can assume that either the joists were too weak for the weight of the house or the joists were green (improperly dried to reduce the moisture content) when they were installed.

**Figure 2-6**
*This square corner indicates that the house has not warped or twisted.*

The results of bowed joists can be seen readily when you get inside the house. You may find spaces between the walls and the flooring because the joists or sills dropped after the flooring was installed. You may also learn that the floors dip in the center of the room or slant badly. If you have questions, lay a small ball or marble on the floor and see if it rolls freely. Give the ball a slight shove. If it rolls away from you and then comes back, there is a definite slant to the floor.

If you can do so, use a chalk line on the floors and even on the walls. Have someone help you by holding the end of the chalk line against the floor at one wall of the room while you stretch the line across the room and hold the end at the floor against the opposite wall. If there are any areas where the line is not in contact with the

floor, you have evidence of sagging of the foundation timbers.

Use the chalk line against the walls to see if the walls have bowed out or in. Try the line from side to side at two or three points along the wall and then from top to bottom. Try the diagonal length of the wall as well.

You may think that this is a great deal of trouble, but keep in mind that you may invest hundreds of dollars in a house that has lost so much integrity that it will be difficult to restore for your family to live in it.

If you have a carpenter's square handy, use it in the corners of rooms. Lay it flat and then stand it on edge to be sure that the walls and floors conform to the square. If the rooms are out of square, you may have more than a small amount of problems later if you decide to install carpet or wall or floor coverings.

Figure 2-6 shows a square held on the corner of a hallway and kitchen wall. The corner is perfectly square, which is a great indication that the house has not warped or twisted.

Make a visual check of the tops of walls where the ceilings meet the walls. Check to see if there are cracks between the ceiling covering and the wall covering. As you walk across the floors, notice whether the floors support you solidly or whether the floors give or sink slightly under your weight.

If possible, go into the attic and check for leaks in the roof. Look under insulation (be sure to wear gloves when you pull back the insulation batt ends) to see if there has been evidence of moisture collecting under the insulation. If there is dampness, the house roof has leaked or there is a condensation problem, either of which will rot roof timbers.

Use your chalk line, level, and screwdriver on the attic timbers. Check the roof rafters and the girders for integrity. Notice whether rafters or joists have had large holes cut through them so that plumbing piles or electrical wiring can be passed through the timbers. If joists or rafters have been weakened, the integrity of the timber has been compromised or damaged.

Don't neglect to check out closets and pantries. Often the large cracks made by weakened timbers or settling can be hidden by wide molding, but most people do not worry about cracks that show up in closets.

But you should worry about them. If the house is vacant, open the closets and check the meeting points of the floor and walls and the ceilings and walls.

If you can arrange to do so, visit the house after or even during a heavy rain. If the house is snug and dry during these times, it is probably sound weather-wise.

When you have finished the interior examination of the house, go outside to check for other potential problems. Notice whether the house is bounded by large trees. Will the mover have to cut the trees in order to move the house? If so, will there be damage to the neighbor's house or lawn or garden? If there will be damage, you may have a problem on your hands, because the neighbor might press charges against you for

**Figure 2-7**
*This house is surrounded by trees and shrubs, making moving it more difficult.*

**Figure 2-8**
*Trees a hundred feet from this house were cut in preparation for its move.*

damage to his house or property. Aesthetic damage is often considered worse than the mere physical damage.

In Figure 2-7 you can see the huge number of trees and shrubs that surround the house. This house, incidentally, was offered free to anyone who would pay to have it moved. Cost of moving was estimated to be $15,000 for a cross-town trip. And while this seems to be a substantial amount of money, keep in mind that the moving fee would barely pay for the addition of a second or third bathroom to your existing house.

Is there a sidewalk that the house must cross? If so, will the weight of the house break or crack the sidewalk, and if it does, will you be legally responsible for the damage?

If the house is dangerously close to other houses, or if the lot is so narrow that the house must be turned to move it up the street, will there be damage to the property of others? Check out all these possibilities before you buy the house.

Drive along the route the house must take. Count the number of power lines, telephone lines, TV cable lines, or any other lines that must be taken down in order for the house to pass up or down the street. Keep in mind that you may have to engage the services of the power company or cable company to send crews out to raise or lower the lines while the house moves past. Often the strategy is to take down one line at a time and replace it as soon as the house has passed. By doing so, you will not disrupt the electrical service or cable service for more than a few minutes at most.

**Figure 2-9**
*This house's chimneys were removed prior to its move, and later rebuilt.*

Notice whether the neighbor's tree limbs hang over into the path of the house. If you must have these limbs cut, will the neighbor insist that you have damaged his trees?

Figure 2-8 shows a moving operation about to begin. Notice that there were many trees a hundred feet from the house, and some of these trees had to be cut. The movers arranged a deal to pay the owners of the trees and the move was made harmoniously.

Try several routes. If you can significantly cut the number of lines to be lowered or raised, you have lessened your costs, even though the alternate route may be a mile or two longer.

The mover will, of course, map out the best route, but if you determine from your own checking that one house may have to pass through extremely difficult areas, you may want to give more consideration to another house.

Drive the entire route. Landmarks along the way that you notice only casually will become major obstacles in many cases when you are moving a house past them. Is there a bridge so narrow that the house will strike the railings? Is there an underpass so low that the house cannot move past it without damage? Is there a busy intersection that will prove to be difficult to negotiate? Are there trees along the route that will be damaged by the house, or will the house be damaged by tree limbs?

What about weight limits for bridges or roads? How much does the house weigh? This is a question that baffles nearly everyone who must face the question.

A rule of thumb is that a frame house will weigh about 20 pounds per square foot, and a brick house will weigh about 40 pounds per square foot. A frame house of 1600 square feet, then, will weigh about 32,000 pounds, and a brick house of the same size will weigh 64,000 pounds.

You must include the weight of upstairs areas also. A two-story house will weigh about twice as much as a single-story house, and you must consider this weight in relation to the capacity of the bridges or highways.

What if the house must pass through the busiest part of the entire town, and the traffic congestion will be a nightmare? Some towns will permit the house to be moved after midnight when there is virtually no traffic.

Are there railroad crossings you must pass over? Some cities prohibit crossing tracks, particularly if the barricades must be taken down

in order to allow the house to cross the tracks. Check out the possibilities before you ever make an offer.

There are other considerations you must or should make relative to the house. If there is a garage, it will need to be taken down or at least

**Figure 2-10**
*All but the top of this house's chimney was left intact for its move.*

separated from the house. If there is a closed-in patio area, this, too, must be moved separately.

If there is a chimney, you should confer with the mover to see whether the chimney can be moved with the house or if it must be taken down and rebuilt on the new site. It *is* possible to move the chimney intact, but consult with a brick mason to find out what his fee would be to rebuild the chimney and then ask the mover what his fee is with and without moving the chimney.

In Figure 2-9 you see a house that was moved after the chimneys were torn down. Then, when the house was at its new site, the chimneys were rebuilt.

In Figure 2-10 you can see a house being moved with the chimney intact. Only the top of the chimney was taken down so that the house could pass under power lines. In such a move, it is much easier to rebuild part of the chimney than it is to pay for the wires that must be taken down and then put back up.

Notice in Figure 2-10 that this house is being moved with the brick siding intact. Such a move goes slowly, and frequent stops must be made to check the load and obstacles that the house meets in transit. Here a curb is being negotiated. Note the front wheels of the cab in the air because of the weight of the house and the slow movement of the haul.

The same fact about chimneys is true of brick siding. An experienced mover can move the house with the bricks intact. Some prefer to take the brick veneer off and then have the house re-bricked on the new site.

Ask for both prices. Assume that you will have to pay $9,500 to have a huge house moved with the bricks still on it, but you can have the house moved for only $7,000 if the bricks are taken off before the move. Then ask a mason

what he will charge to brick the house after it is delivered. If he agrees to do it for $1,500, then you can save $1,000 by having the bricks removed. If the mason asks $3,000, then you will lose money and you should let the mover transport the house with the bricks intact.

Keep in mind that the figures quoted here and elsewhere in this book are merely working figures. You must check with movers in your area for more exact costs.

Assuming you have a number of houses to choose from, how do you make the final choice and still get the most for your money? There are some obviously easy answers. If the house is almost new and in meticulous condition, and if you can buy it for only $1,000 or so more than a 50-year old house in moderately good condition will cost, then go with the new house. If the new house is $10,000 and you can buy an older house in excellent shape for $50, then by all means go with the bargain-basement house.

**Figure 2-11**
*Moving the House of the Seven Gables presented a formidable challenge.*

Keep in mind that houses built a century ago may well be better houses than those constructed six months ago. A hundred years ago heart pine was often used for sills and joists and girders, and these timbers are strong, durable, and seasoned perfectly even today. Many houses built a year ago contain studs weakened by knots and other defects, and the larger timbers are often of a lower grade of wood. The older houses may have real oak paneling, while newer ones may contain plywood veneer.

Newer houses will likely have better plumbing and wiring, but older houses may have tile roofing which is nearly priceless, while newer ones may have low-grade shingles. The reverse may also be true: older houses may have inferior materials. In short, if the house was superb in its day, it is probably still superb, despite its rough edges. If it was made of inferior materials, no matter when it was built, it is no bargain.

Size is an important factor. It is very true that enormous houses can be moved. The House of the Seven Gables, made famous in Hawthorne's classic novel, was moved from its original site in Salem to the present location where it is maintained by the federal government. If this house can be moved, considering its age and size, most houses today can be moved. See Figure 2-11 to get an idea of the size of the marvelous old House of the Seven Gables.

It is possible to move buildings of six, eight, or even 10 stories. The Cape Hatteras lighthouse on North Carolina's Outer Banks, the tallest lighthouse in the United States, will be moved soon, to give another illustration of the nearly miraculous engineering that is possible. See Figure 2-12.

But obviously it is easier and therefore cheaper to move a smaller house than a huge house. Single-floored structures are easier and cheaper to move than two-story houses.

**Figure 2-12**
*Even the tallest lighthouse in the United States can be moved!*

So, all things being equal as far as the condition of the house is concerned, if a smaller house will serve you well, buy it and have it moved. If you really need a huge house, then put the bargain attitude out of your head and go with the larger one.

Another consideration is whether you plan to live in the house yourself or rent it. One excellent money-making tactic, to be discussed in more detail later, is that of buying and moving a large number of houses and then reconditioning them to sell or to rent.

So what is the best house for you to buy and move? Put your money on the house that suits your needs and your bank account best. Move the house that will meet your demands now and in the future. If I were faced with moving a house today, I'd go for the biggest and the best I could afford, as long as the house could be moved safely and for a reasonable fee.

If I could buy House A, move it and set it up for living again, and the $5,000 investment grew to a $50,000 value within six months, or House B with its $10,000 investment and its $200,000 value within six months, I'd go with House B, if my budget could stand it. Where else can you increase your investment by 20 times in such a short time period and with virtually no risk?

But in order to help you with the decision, I discuss a lengthy series of other considerations in the following chapters. Chapter Three discusses the all-important question of how much you can expect to pay for the house itself.

# Chapter Three
# How Much Should You Pay?

In the Introduction to this book I described how we bought our house to move for less than $1. Before discussing how much or how little you can expect to pay, it might be well to share two or three factual incidents with you.

A man read in the newspaper that the air strip at the local airport would be extended, and the construction would require the removal of three hundred houses in a development. Interested in the possibility that he could buy a house cheaply and have it moved, the man visited the houses and noticed that there were residential dwellings of every reasonable size and style. Some obviously were worth many thousands of dollars, while others were modest at best.

The houses were to be sold at a sealed-bid auction, so the person who offered the highest price for any particular house was the official buyer. The man went from house to house, finding some characteristics he liked in nearly all of them and yet not finding the perfect house.

So he conceived a brilliant solution: he placed a bid of $25 on each house in the entire development. He reasoned (correctly, as it turned out), that he would perhaps buy at least one of the houses. If he bought more than one, he could afford to lose his $25 deposit, or he could in turn sell the house to someone else for $50 and double his modest investment.

He was the high bidder on dozens of the houses! When the bids were opened, airport officials learned that the man was the *only bidder* on dozens of the houses. Other people had gone in and placed bids on the biggest, most beautiful, and most expensive houses, and the large numbers of mid-range houses were totally disregarded.

Now what was he to do? He had obligated himself to spend more than $1,250 for the houses, and as he reasoned it, he decided that even if he had paid that amount for only one house, it was still a bargain.

So he hired a mover to load up the first $25 house and haul it to the man's property. As the house was being hauled through town, it had to stop at a busy intersection while traffic was directed around it. A motorist stopped beside the house and the truck that was pulling it and asked if the house was for sale.

"I'll give you $40,000 for it," the motorist said when he learned that the house was indeed on the market (although it had not been seconds earlier).

The owner and the motorist drew up an agreement and the new owner directed the truck driver to the motorist's property. Now the man who had bought the house had multiplied his investment by 1600 times within a few hours, and the motorist agreed to pay for the moving costs.

So the man who made the successful bids on the houses directed the mover to deposit the first house on the motorist's lot and to return to move another house. This time he moved the house to the location intended for the first house, and by this time he had decided to buy his own house-moving equipment and go into business for himself.

**Figures 3-1, 3-2, and 3-3**
*Houses like these can be found readily and bought for a very small amount of money.*

He moved the houses to his property, paid crews to build foundation walls and to restore the houses to their original condition, and then the buyer sold the houses for fees roughly comparable to the original ones.

A man in another part of the country profited $600,000 within little more than two months, simply by doing the same thing the first man had done: place a bid on each and every house. Figures 3-1, 3-2, and 3-3 show the kinds of houses that are available when huge building projects are started.

In another house-moving deal, a house had stood empty for several months. A large and beautiful house in superb shape, the residence stood in the way of a highway project and had to be moved or torn down. The state had paid the original owners the full value of the house, and the owners had in turn bought the house back from the state at a sealed-bid sale. Now the owners wanted to get a few dollars profit out of their house and placed it on the market.

A businessman saw the house and contacted the owners. He offered $1,200 for the house and the owners accepted the offer instantly. The new owner hired movers to transport the house two miles down the road, and he had the house bricked and re-done inside and out. He invested several thousands of dollars in the $1,200 house and when the work was completed he had a house that was easily worth $300,000.

In this particular case, the buyer cost himself a thousand dollars because of his too-high bid.

What the buyer did not know was that the owners had offered the house for sale for $500 for months and there had been no takers. Still, because of the great house he bought, he realized one of the best bargains imaginable. Figure 3-4 shows the house (also seen in Figure 3-3) as it was being prepared for the move.

Notice in Figure 3-4 that the foundation walls have been taken from under the house and the house now rests on steel beams to which axles and wheels will be attached for the move. Notice, too, that the high porch pillars have been removed and the roof of the porch is supported by temporary bracing that will be

**Figure 3-4**
*A beautiful old house being prepared to move.*

taken down later, after the house has been delivered to its new location.

In a third incident a pair of young people decided to get married, and the bride's father bought a house for $300 and paid $800 to have it moved to the lot where the couple would reside. The customers then hired carpenters and masons to add brick siding and beautiful fireplaces in the den and basement that had been dug before the house was moved.

When the house was completed, the couple owned a house worth many times what they paid for it. Unless the house can be bought and moved for very little, or unless you can see great potential value in the house when it is restored, you might be better off to look else-where. In this case the investment was a sound one and the house has increased in value every year since it was moved. See Figure 3-5 for a look at the moved and restored house. Figure 3-6 shows the fireplaces in the basement of the house.

**Figure 3-5**
*A house bought for nearly nothing and restored to a state of near-perfection.*

So we have seen three stories with widely varying results. The first man played the game wisely and bought at a low price and sold at a comparatively high price and became wealthy. The second man invested more but still he received a tremendous bargain. The third man spent a fairly large amount of money on a house that was worth comparatively little, but he managed to get a great bargain for his investment.

So what does this tell you about how much you should pay? It offers suggestions as to what to do or what not to do. And here are several other suggestions that may prove to be of value to you.

First, when you see the sign proclaiming the site to be the future home of a fast-food restaurant, you know that the people who will build the new eatery face two choices: they can sell the house on the property and perhaps realize a small return on their initial investment, or they can pay to have the house demolished and hauled away.

If I were a potential buyer, I would first meet with a house mover and learn what he would charge me to move the house to my property. If he quoted me an esti-mate of $6,000 or so, I would then approach the owners of the house and make an offer to clear the old house off the lot and therefore save the owners the huge expense of hiring a demolition crew.

I would offer to re-move the house from the premises and clear the lot for $7,500. If the owners accepted, I'd engage the services of the house movers and I would make myself a tidy profit of $1,500 on the deal. Seen another way, the house would lack $1,500 of costing me anything.

If the owners did not accept my offer, I'd lower my fee for clearing the lot. If worse came to worst, I'd finally offer to clear the lot if they agreed to give me the house at no charge.

My suggestion to you is to take much the same approach. Do not appear too eager to get the house. Offer to clear the old hulk off the property for a stated fee. Only as a last resort should you agree to pay for the house.

The same principle holds true for houses on lots inherited by churches, colleges, or other institutions who could have no possible use for the dwelling.

If there is only one isolated house available, I'd offer a very small amount: $100 or less. In fact, I'd first ask for the owners to give me the house and offer cash only when the owners flatly refused to deal with me otherwise.

So what should you pay?

My suggestion is that unless the house is one of exceptional beauty or intrinsic value, I would never go beyond $500. There are entirely too many houses available for you to pay a high price for one.

If the house is nearly new, the workmanship is great, and the house cost $150,000 to build a year ago, then I'd raise my offer considerably. For a house of that sort, you could easily bid $10,000 up to $20,000, depending upon the cost of moving the house. Determine that first.

If the house was an old dwelling that was in fair shape at best, my high bid would be $150. If it was a two-story house of 4,000 square feet, I'd bid no more than $25 to $50. My logic would be that the house will cost a great deal to move, and there are few people interested in the house in the first place.

All of these considerations are, of course, subject to varying circumstances. If the mover offers you a great deal, you can afford to pay more, if you must, for the house.

You should also take into consideration how much the total house cost will be. Don't think only in terms of buying the house as it stands on the property of someone else. The house is not yours until it is on your property and paid for.

When you get an estimate from the mover, then make a quick calculation on the costs of foundation walls, wiring and plumbing connections, re-bricking, if necessary, and all the other costs associated with setting the house back up as a residence.

Assume for the moment that the cost of the house on the other person's lot is $3,000

**Figure 3-6**
*Basement of house shown in previous illustration.*

(which, incidentally, is far more than I would pay for anything but a near-mansion), and the mover's cost is $7,000 (also high for an uncomplicated move). You already have $10,000 tied up in the house.

Cost of foundation walls will be $1,200 (this, too, is only a guess; it depends upon which masons you hire and on what basis they are hired), so your tab is now $11,200. Assume that it will cost $3,000 to have the chimney rebuilt, so you are up to $14,200 and counting.

If it costs you another $4,000 to have the wiring and plumbing connected, and if you must dig a septic tank and well, assuming that the house is in the country, you can add another $3,000 or so to the cost, so you are at $21,200. If the costs of minor repairs are $3,000, you are now at $24,200.

Now, how much would the same house cost you if you were to buy it and the land it stands on? Could you get it for $50,000? If so, you are still better off moving and refurbishing it than if you had decided to buy the house and lot and be done with the deal. You have saved about $25,000, which is a lot of dollars.

But take the same house and run the figures another way. You get the house for nearly nothing: $200. Your moving cost is still $7,000, but you hire the other work done through the suggestions made in a following chapter or you make a special deal, also described in the following pages, and your total cost for the house and moving and restoration is about $9,500. Now you have really made a deal. You have the bargain of a lifetime.

You still have the cost of the land and of septic tank and well, unless you hook onto a city or county system, but even with the added costs you have a whale of a bargain. And you should keep in mind the fact that you must pay for a well and septic tank, if you are living in the country, no matter whether you move a house, have one built, or live in a mobile home. You will also have the cost of land in any event.

What are these special deals mentioned earlier? These include, but are not limited to, the point-to-point move versus the turnkey job. You also have a wide range of options for the other work. These will be discussed in detail.

In our particular case, our total bill was less than $15,000 for a house evaluated at $80,000 at first, then at $100,000. But keep in mind that our $14,000 cost included moving the house, setting it up for residency, well, septic tank, furniture, and 24 acres of beautiful land.

The land itself was worth far more than the total cost, even if the house had not been included. There are also suggestions on how to buy land, if you have not already done so, in the Loompanics Unlimited book *How To Buy Land Cheap*.

For the present, think only of how much to pay for the house as it stands, and keep your sights on $500 or less. You should make an effort to pay a flat zero if possible, or even get paid to take the house off the land. For more details, read on. The next chapter deals with the costs of moving and setting up the house.

# Chapter Four
# Setting Up the Move

*What does it cost to have a house moved?* This is the most frequently asked question I hear on the topic, and the answer is always the same: What kind of house, what size, what kind of move, how far, how complicated, and what firm is moving it?

As stated earlier, huge houses cost more to move, as a rule, than do small houses. Brick costs more than frame. And where you live in the nation determines in part what your cost will be. If you live in the middle of New York City or Chicago, Los Angeles, San Francisco, Houston, or Jacksonville, your cost will likely be much greater than if you live in Raton, New Mexico, Flagstaff, Arizona, Montpelier, Vermont, or Jackman, Maine.

If you live in North Carolina, South Carolina, Georgia, Tennessee, or Kentucky, your cost will possibly be less than in any other part of the country. Still, the man who owns the house-moving equipment is the one who makes the final decision based on the degree of complications in the move and how much profit he intends to make on the deal.

When we moved our house, the first mover said the house was too big to move down 18 miles of busy highway. The second mover said the house could be moved but it would cost us $8,000. The third said he could move it for $2,500 and guarantee in writing that the house would not be damaged in transit.

Now that's a large differential. By hiring the third mover, we saved $5,500. But we moved our house several years ago, and costs have gone up dramatically, right?

Not necessarily. The second man we talked with said only months ago that he could move a house like ours the same distance for half of what he quoted us before we hired the third man. What I don't understand is whether costs of moving a house dropped in the interim (the mover says that costs of moving have indeed gone down, rather than up, in recent months) or whether he decided that if he had a second chance, he'd settle for less profit than he thought he'd make on the first estimate.

I tend to think in terms of the latter. I believe that the man who moved our house earned and made a profit, just as I am confident the second man could have also made a profit if he had taken the job for half his estimated cost.

So you will have to shop around, just as you would if you were buying a new car or hiring someone to roof your house. The extra time you spend in shopping around may well pay off in savings of hundreds or even thousands of dollars.

**Figure 4-1**
*One of the inexpensive moves.*

**Figure 4-2**
*This is obviously a costly house to move.*

**Figure 4-3**
*The beautiful old house is being moved along one of the busiest stretches
of highway in the area.*

The cheapest price I have heard for moving a full-sized house is $800. The house was a two-bedroom structure with kitchen, den, small dining room, and one and a half baths. The move was a very easy one in a tiny town and along a street where no wires had to be taken down or raised.

The most expensive move I have encountered was well over the $20,000 mark, but the house being moved was the biggest I have ever seen moved in the private sector. It contained well over 10,000 square feet, and the move was highly complicated. See Figures 4-1 and 4-2 for examples of an inexpensive house to move and one that was costly to move.

The house being moved in Figure 4-3 is one of the largest houses I have ever seen actually in transit down the busiest highway in the county. It is often not simply the size of the house but the traffic patterns involved that complicate the move. In this case the traffic was great enough that the mover had to make use of several highway patrolmen and sheriff's deputies, and a huge number of wires had to be taken down and put back up.

The house was delivered to the site and then the owner hired a crew to brick the house's exterior and change its entire appearance. By doing so he created one of the most beautiful houses in the area. Figure 4-4 shows the house as it appears today.

When you discuss the cost of moving, ask the mover about the point-to-point job and the turnkey job. There will be a large difference in the cost of the two, and you will need to decide which is your best deal.

A point-to-point job, as the term implies, simply means that the house mover will load the

**Figure 4-4**
*Here is the same house as it has been completely re-done.*

house "onto the steel" at the point of origin, and he will deliver the house to your lot and will back it into the exact position you want. At this point he will lower the house onto huge cross-stacked timbers or other supports and he will drive away, after first picking up your check.

From that point on it is up to you to take care of all of the details, and that includes foundation walls, wiring, and anything else that needs to be done. When the house is ready, you will call the mover and he will come back and lower the house onto the foundation walls, pick up his timbers, and leave. The house is now yours. Figure 4-5 shows a house that was bought for, as the mover put it, "a song, and it was sung out of tune," and moved in a point-to-point arrangement. The customer had to pay for the work of setting up the house for residence. Final cost of the entire house was less than that of a very modest mobile home.

**Figure 4-5**
*A sample of house that can be bought, moved, and restored for a very small investment.*

The turnkey job is almost the exact opposite. You make the deal, and the mover will load the house, deliver it, and then do all of the work needed so that you can move into the house. He will take care of painting, wiring, plumbing, bricking, chimney work, and anything else that needs to be done, short of mowing your lawn.

Here are the basic pros and cons of the two types of moves. In the point-to-point job you save a great deal of money during the actual moving. You may elect to hire someone to do the work after the mover leaves, and you may strike a deal that will save you money over the long run. You may even choose to do much or all of the work yourself. So you save dollars, but the deal will cost you more in your time and sweat.

The turnkey job is far more expensive, but you are spared the frustration, the bother, the long hours of work, and all the other aggravation that accompanies the work.

Which is better? It depends upon how much money you have to spend, or what levels of skills you can bring to the job if you decide to do it yourself.

When we moved our house, we chose the point-to-point deal, and we think it was the right one. We saw several advantages from the beginning. First, if the mover had done a turnkey job, we'd have owed him a rather large sum of money at one whack. Instead, we paid him $2,500 and we were through with him. Then, in the days and weeks following, we could buy cement blocks and mortar and pay for the expenses in small, easy payments. If we chose to hire a mason, we could pay him when he completed the work. In other words, the payments are spaced far enough apart that they are not as painful as they would be if you paid a lump sum.

Another advantage in our case was that we could do nearly all of the required work in our spare time. So I did not lose work time at the office or salary, and I did not owe half of every paycheck to some worker.

Perhaps the greatest advantage was that when we did the work, we knew that it was done honestly and close to being right. We encountered horror stories involving people who were hired to do the work in the houses of friends, and we were determined that if we were going to be robbed, the thief would at least have to point a gun at us.

In view of everything, the point-to-point arrangement seems to be the better bet for the typical person who wants to buy and move a house. However, if you don't feel competent to handle the work involved, and there is a degree of work that must be done, here are some alternative suggestions.

Make the turnkey deal with the understanding that the mover will hire you to work for him in setting up the house. Have it understood that you will do only that work which you are able to do effectively, and have it understood that he will not pay you a cash wage but simply permit you to work off some of the money you will owe him.

For example, if you can't lay blocks for the foundation wall, can you at least mix the concrete for the masons who do the actual block work? Can you work as a carpenter's assistant if there is carpentry work to be done? If you can drive a nail, saw a straight line, lift a board, and use a tape measure and square, you could learn to do a great deal of the necessary work.

At first, before I realized that my wife and I could do the work effectively, I worked for the mason when we did the work on our house. My jobs were to mix the concrete for the footings (the mason told me exactly what mixtures to use), and I dumped the concrete into a wheelbarrow and hauled it to the work site.

I also found a way to work that was extremely hard on me but very easy on my bank account. When I first mentioned that I would like to work at mixing concrete and mortar, the mason laughed until he was gasping for breath. He said that there was no college teacher in the country who could do the work and keep up with him.

So I worked like a demon, and then I tried to make it seem easy. When I rounded the corner away from him, I literally ran with the wheelbarrow to the mixer. I shoveled as if my life depended upon it, and then I pushed the wheelbarrow at top speed back to the corner. When I rounded it again, I slowed to a near-crawl, whistled, and in general acted as if this was the easiest work I had ever done.

I sweated profusely as I carried bricks and other materials to him, and when I squeezed out a few seconds I dashed to the truck and poured

him a glass of iced tea. And the easier I made the job seem, the more determined the mason was to kill me. So he worked harder and harder, and he finished the job in less than one-half the estimated time. I saved fifty per cent of the money I would have owed him.

Later I was able to use a trowel and smoother to work the concrete smooth, and I helped to drive the stakes and lay out the guidelines. The mason explained that he would have paid a helper $8.50 an hour, and as it worked out he didn't have to pay me the salary and I didn't have to pay for the assistant or labor.

Later, when we progressed to laying the blocks for foundation walls, I mixed and hauled mortar to the work site. I also carried blocks to the mason and placed them so that all he had to do was lay one block, reach down to pick up another, then lay another and another. There was never a time he did not have blocks and mortar at his fingertips, and the result was that the work went smoothly and rapidly.

When we reached a certain point, by mutual agreement, I was to take over the rest of the work. The mason's job was to lay the corners, which are the crucial points, and all I had to do was fill in between the corners. So I borrowed a portable mixer and my wife and I completed the foundation walls without difficulty.

I estimated that I saved at least $900 in salary by working for myself, and we learned that we could handle most or all of the later work in that area of expertise.

We decided we wanted a full basement for our house, and since it is impossible to move the basement, we had no choice but to dig the basement after the house was in place. We hired a man with the necessary heavy equipment, and he came in and burrowed under the house. Within hours, the basement excavation was complete.

My wife and I then set about pouring the concrete floor for the basement. We checked out a book on the subject from the library and we went to work. First, we had loads of gravel and sand and bags of cement delivered to our house site. We laid off the floor to the thickness that we wanted, covered the bottom with three inches of sand, and then added three inches of gravel on top of the sand. Then we covered the gravel with thick plastic, and we poured the concrete on top of the plastic. We made the concrete floor five inches thick, and as we worked, I mixed and poured and my wife smoothed (the screeding part of the job) the surface to the desired state.

The two of us completed the entire basement floor. When we were finished, we had torrential rains, and the floor never leaked at all. Nor did it crack.

Then we laid the basement walls. Because the foundation walls for the house were already laid and the house was sitting on the walls, we were afraid to dig too close to the walls for fear of damaging them, so we laid our basement walls three feet inside the foundation walls.

This turned out to be an excellent idea, for the dead air space between walls helped to both heat the house and cool it, and also gave us a double-strong foundation. We left openings from the basement to the space between walls, and this turned out to be the perfect place to store our crops of potatoes and other items that needed a cool, dry place.

We completed the basement walls without the slightest degree of difficulty. It was hard work, but we did a good job and we saved hundreds of dollars.

As the rest of the work was done, we pitched in and either did the work or helped with the work. In either case, we saved large amounts of money.

Here is a second suggestion. If you cannot hire the work done because plumbers and electricians charge far too much (Remember the old joke about the lawyer who received the bill from the plumber and screamed that the amount was more than the lawyer earned in a week? The plumber replied that it was more than he earned, too, when he was a lawyer.), there is another possibility.

Check with the local college or university maintenance staff. Or with the high school or elementary school staff. These schools cannot afford to call in an electrician or plumber each time they need repair work done, so they hire a staff member or members who are licensed in these fields but who do not wish to work full time in either area. The other members of the staff are either licensed or skilled in the required areas.

Ask them if they would like to do some moonlighting for you. They will not expect to receive the pay rate that plumbers of electricians receive, and you can save a huge amount of money while these workers earn their holiday cash or vacation money.

The third suggestion is to do the work yourself, except for the more technical parts of it. Throughout this chapter I have stressed saving large amounts of money. This does not mean that you will be spending thousands and thousands of dollars if you do not help to do the work. But my assumption is that you are not incredibly wealthy or you would not be moving a house. You'd pay cash for one and get on with your life.

If you are like me, you want and need to earn and save money whenever possible and practical. But if you elect to hire the work done and pay for every minute of it, you still will not spend a large amount of money in the real sense.

The beauty of it all is that the money you spend can be viewed as mortgage payments. You don't send a check to the bank each month for thirty years; instead, you send one check to the electrician, another to the roofer, and one to the mason.

And then you are through. You have only three "mortgage" payments, and then the house is yours.

Of course, if you wish you can borrow the money to have the house moved and set up for residence. Then you can pay off the money as you would any short-term loan. But you are better off if you do not have to borrow at all. I have always viewed interest as money thrown away, except when there is no way to avoid borrowing money for emergencies.

A final suggestion, if time is important, is to hire the skilled people you need only for as long as it takes you to get into the house as a resident. Get the basic wiring connections made, the septic tank hooked up, and the foundation wall built. If there is a chimney, get it built. Get the heating and cooling systems operative. You should be able to use the ones that were in the house when you moved it. When all of this is done, and when the building inspector has approved the house (you may not need to call the building inspector at all, but you should check before you move too far and too fast) so that you can move in, do so. Then, in your spare time, take care of the other items that are not pressing.

You may at this time still be apprehensive, so in the next chapter you will find information that should be soothing to you. This information deals with insurance, financing, building permits, tax valuations on your house, and other pertinent matters relative to money and your house.

# Chapter Five
# The Paperwork in
# House Moving

Anyone who thinks about moving a house will devote many long minutes or even hours to pondering the questions of financing, insurance, building inspections, and all the other red tape that is part of the American scene. This chapter is intended to bring information and relief.

First, as for financing, many banks will refuse to lend money to finance the moving of a house, but this attitude is not a dead end; in fact, it is an open door. Many insurance firms will be reluctant to insure a house that is being moved, but this, too, is another door which, if not open, is revolving.

Be sure to check the policies and laws in your own state or even city or county before you become too deeply involved with a mover. Or have the mover, your banker, or the insurance company offer counsel and advice. Here's how it works in many states and with many banks and insurance companies.

While many banks will not lend money on a house to be moved, they will willingly lend money on a house that *has been* moved. And while many insurance companies will not cover a house *to be* moved, they will insure a house that *has been* moved.

So where does that leave you? First, the house mover must be insured according to state laws in many if not all states. So your house is fully covered while it is being jacked up in preparation to being hauled away. Your house is covered while it is on the highway, so if there is a mishap, you are not left to suffer.

When your house is deposited on the crossbeam supports on your own lot, then your insurance takes effect. You can in many instances buy construction insurance to cover the house while you are preparing it for residency.

As suggested earlier, the same is true of financing. The mover unhooks your house and leaves it on your lot, and at this point it is a permanent house, just as any and all other houses on your street or highway are permanent houses. At this point you can finance the house, and you can use part of the money to pay the mover, who already understands how the system works and will usually cooperate with you.

The reason for stating that "many banks" and "many insurance" companies will act in a certain way is to keep from making a blanket statement. I have called banks and insurance companies in several states from the East Coast to the West Coast, and they have all said essentially what I have said above. That does not, however, mean that you cannot find a bank or insurance carrier that will not act in the same manner. Check it out before you authorize the deal.

What about tax valuation? Again, in *many* areas the cost of a building permit is based on the cost of completing the work on the house. In other areas the square footage is the key. In our case, the cost of the permit was based on the cost of the house. Because we were going to spend only about $10,000, give or take a few dollars, our building permit was virtually free.

And because our house cost so little to complete, it was seen by the tax assessor as being worth only that amount of money. So we paid $25 a year in tax for years after our house was moved and restored. Yet the insurance company readily agreed to provide us with full coverage on our place of residence.

So we, in essence, enjoyed the best of two worlds.

What about the resale value of a moved house? One realtor told us, "We consider a house that has been moved to be equally as valuable as a house that was constructed on the spot."

But isn't there a great deal of damage to a house that is being jacked up, loaded on a steel carriage to which wheels have been bolted and aligned, and then carried over bumps, railroad tracks, and plowed fields? Isn't the integrity of the house weakened by all the stress and swaying, starting and stopping?

"We hear the same question regularly," a North Carolina house mover told me. "And I tell them that a house that has been moved is not only as strong as a house that has not been moved, it is usually much stronger. I assure them that the structural integrity of a moved house is greater than one that has remained on the spot where it was constructed."

How can this be? A series of house movers responded to this question. Their answers have been summarized below.

If a house was built 20 years ago, or even five years ago, it has stood on the same location all that time. If the footings were not deep enough, or if the soil was too soft, or if it shifted over the

months, then one corner of the house may have sunk more than the other end, and the result was uneven floors, out-of-square corners, windows and doors that either refused to open or refused to close, and cabinets with sprung doors.

When the house was jacked up in preparation for the move, the jacks operated in unison. The old color-coded jacks were marked so that the operators were assured of an even lift on all parts of the house. This means that the low corners are raised until they are level with the formerly high corners. This means that the beams and supports that had tended to warp or twist or bend were coaxed back into their original positions and shapes.

While the house is jacked up and while it is perfectly level and while the corners are again square, reinforcements are added to the corners to keep them square. Many building materials and techniques seldom if ever used only a few years ago are now commonly employed, and your house is improved by the use of such items as plywood or metal corner bracing, and by much stricter enforcement of the building codes.

As for the stress of swaying and bumping, one mover stated it like this: "When the house is on the steel, it does not travel as you do in the seat of a car. In the family car you may get jostled and thrown about on rough terrain. But the house rides as though it were on a boat or ship. No matter how much the ship pitches and tosses, the deck remains essentially stable. So does the house, and it rides easily and safely over curbs, railway tracks, and fields."

What about damage to the house along the way? "We take the house on such a smooth ride that there are few rough spots," the mover said. "In one house that we moved someone had left a pot of beans on the kitchen range. No one thought to remove it. We reached the final point of the trip and set the house down, and when we stepped inside we realized that not one bean had been spilled."

Another mover reported that it is extremely rare for even a pane of glass to be cracked in transit. This may be difficult to believe, but when you have seen how skillful a professional mover can be, you'll have your own praises to sing about them. When our house was moved, I dreamed the night before that I was coming home from the college where I taught and I saw boards and rafters and broken windows littering both sides of the highway. To my immense relief, when I arrived home the house arrived safely, with no damage whatsoever.

In some cases the buyer can purchase the furnishings of the house; in many other cases the drapes and wall coverings and decorations are sometimes seen as now being a permanent part of the house and will be left in place.

At this point several surprising advantages of house moving should be clear: there is little damage, if any, likely; you can finance the house just as you would finance a house built on the location; you can insure your house once it arrives, and en route it will be insured by the mover, under nearly all circumstances; you can get an inexpensive builder's permit because of the small cost of the structure you will complete or have completed; the taxes on the house will be generally low, if your county bases the rate on value rather than square footage; and when the house is completed, it is impossible to tell a moved house from one that was constructed on-site.

To further ease your apprehensions, call the mover and set up an appointment. Go to his place of business and talk with him. Learn the names of people whose houses he has moved and then call the people and go see their houses. Ask the mover to alert you when he plans to move another house, and he will likely invite you to drive by the site and watch — from a safe distance — how the entire operation is handled. You can watch the old house as it is prepared for the move, and you can imagine how the house you buy will look as it undergoes the transformation.

You can see the house as it is loaded onto the steel and wheels, and you can even watch it as it

moves into the street and heads for its new location. Then you can watch as it is set back up as a residence.

A word of warning: the scene is often not a pretty one. We who see only the completed house or the house under construction tend to forget how portions of that same neat house look after a few years. When the house has its brick veneer or siding, when the foundation walls are in place, the neatness factor is unchanged. But when you see the old timbers and the shocking variations in color, you may be shocked.

Don't let this appearance confuse you. It is still the same house, and if you had bought it and moved in it where it stands, you would never see the undesirable parts. You are simply looking at the ravages of time — like comparing a high school photo with the man who graduated, 20 years later.

One highly interesting aspect of house moving is that in some towns and cities there are the residential equivalent of used-car lots. Some movers locate houses to be moved, buy them, and move them to huge lots where potential buyers can come and look at the houses, walk through them, and then perhaps put a down payment on them.

The dealer will then deliver the house to your property, and you can proceed with the business of preparing it for family living. You will pay more at one of the house lots than you are likely to pay to an individual owner, but you will save money on the moving end of the deal, in all probability.

Not only that, you will be able to see that the house can be and has been moved safely. There is a comfort in knowing that the dwelling is sturdy enough to withstand the move and not suffer as a result.

Another beauty of the house lots is that you will have several "makes and models" to choose from, just as you would on the used-car lot. You can look at ranch style, A-frame in some cases, two-story, tri-level, duplex, and other architectural styles and models. You can see the size of rooms, the amount of light admitted by windows, and derive some notion of how the house would look on your land. You can see the exposed plumbing under the house, and you will know if the pipes are in generally good condition. Wiring is also visible in parts of the house.

Before you settle on a particular house, you might be able to talk to a banker and an insurance agent and persuade them to accompany you on a visit to the house. The agent can likely tell you if there will be any difficulty at all in securing the needed coverage on the house. Some firms, for example, shy away from insuring houses that are beyond a certain number of years in age. They dislike hundred-year old houses; at least, some of them do.

The banker can tell you if he foresees any trouble in making you a loan. He could also be helpful in estimating the worth of the house as it stands and what it will be worth when it is restored as a private dwelling.

You can also check on whether certain government loans are available. And if this seems like a lot of driving and unproductive time spent, keep in mind that you would drive to several car lots before purchasing a car, and you might visit a dozen stores before you bought a pair of shoes. Think how much more important the purchase of a house can be.

When you have completed your investigative work and decide to make the purchase, you are ready to decide whether to choose the turnkey route or the point-to-point approach. The following chapter deals with the two choices. Some brief discussion will be offered on removing the brick veneer or keeping it, and what the basic advantages and disadvantages are to each approach.

Perhaps most importantly, you will see in the following pages detailed discussions on steps you can take to do the actual work yourself if you choose the point-to-point approach.

# Chapter Six
# Turnkey and Point-to-Point Moves: Some Pointers

No matter what anyone tells you, there are wonderful advantages to either style of moving strategy, and there are a few disadvantages. You can move a barn, an ancient log cabin, a motel, a small hospital, or a two-hundred-year-old plantation house. Each of the buildings will suffer slightly during the move, and all will benefit greatly from it. Figure 6-1 shows a complicated municipal move, while Figure 6-2 depicts the moving of an immense rural house. Either can be moved as a point-to-point or as a turnkey deal.

If you select the turnkey option, you will, as already noted, pay more. This is only natural and reasonable. The mover will be spending a great deal more time; he will incur greater expenses in time involved and salaries he must pay; and he will logically expect you to provide the wages he needs.

There is another slight problem. This type of move may be interrupted if the weather or other pressing reasons obligate the mover to leave your house for the moment and move others while the weather permits. You may offset this problem by having a written agreement that he will have his crew of inside workers at your house and that it will be ready for occupancy within a specified period of time or by a certain

date. If he fails, he will be assessed a legal penalty on a per-day basis.

A word of caution: Unless you agreed to do so at the outset, do not pay the mover any money at all until the job is completed or until the terms of the contract are met. He might want you to pay one-third of the moving cost when he begins work, another third when the house is on the road to its new location, and the final third when the work is completed.

Generally speaking and from a purely personal viewpoint, I would not pay any money at all until the heavy equipment is on the scene and the exhaust fumes fill the air. This is not to suggest that a truly professional mover will attempt to stonewall you, but some unscrupulous and enterprising movers might be tempted to take your first check and then delay starting work on the job for weeks or even months.

Some might even ask you to pay the entire amount when the mover starts work. Do not even consider this. At the outside, you might consider paying half when the work begins and half when the job is completed to your total satisfaction, but I would agree to even this deal only if I had little or no choice.

This same pay principle extends to the crew you hire for the completion of the point-to-point work. Agree either to pay the crew by the hour or by the job. If they work by the hour, try to be on hand as much as possible to see that they indeed work and do not take mini-vacations at your expense.

If at all possible, do all the buying of materials for the job. Some jackleg carpenters enjoy over-buying, and others are very careless with the materials once they are purchased. If you are on the job with them, you can stop the masons from dumping thousands of bricks under the house and then charging you for the bricks they did not lay and forcing you to buy more bricks to take the place of those discarded. This is particularly important if you are paying by the bricks laid or by the blocks laid.

If you are on the scene, you can also stop the carpenter who needs a one-foot length of timber and cuts it from the 20 foot 2 x 12 you were saving for that special need later. Some workers prefer to cut the timber at hand so that they will not have to take three or four steps to get a more suitable one, no matter how wasteful the move may be.

If you buy the materials yourself, you can forestall the temptation on the part of the workers to buy the extra panels of plywood or superfluous boards that they drop off at their house before they transport the rest to your house.

If this sounds accusatory, I have personally known people who have, as incredible as it may seem, built entire houses with the over-bought supplies for a series of other customers.

**Figure 6-1**
*A complicated (and expensive) municipal move.*

**Figure 6-2**
*Moving a huge rural house.*

Many builders regularly over-buy by 20% or even 25%, and they keep the overage.

You will have to expect about a 10% waste on most materials, but be wary if the percentage rises higher. Each time a board or other building material unit is damaged or ruined, the carpenter is taking money off your hip or from your bank account.

In nearly all cases, the professional carpenter will not even consider taking unfair advantage of you; it is the fly-by-nighters who play the con games.

When you have hired your own crews, by no means should you ever pay them before the previously agreed-upon time. If you pay by the job, pay one-third when the job is one-third done; another third at the half-way point, and the final third when the job is complete. There are too many horror stories of people who are asked to pay in advance and then never see the workers again.

Remember: If these people worked in a mill, they would not get their first week's pay until they had worked at least one week. No boss is likely to pay workers in advance, and neither should you.

Never, never open an account at the lumber yard or building supply house and permit the crew to charge items to the account. This may sound like elementary advice, but you would be astonished at the number of people who are victimized by unscrupulous and unsavory characters.

Keep the work relationship on a business-like footing. Do not become pals with the workers. You can reprimand your worker and demand high standards, but you are not permitted to criticize or prod a buddy. Do not make the fatal mistake of starting to buy and provide sandwiches and drinks for the workers. If you start it, they will expect you to continue it. Let them bring their own bag lunches or drive to the local fast-food eatery for their noon meals.

Back to the house work. If you plan to move a brick-veneered house, remember that you have two choices: You can move it with the bricks on it, which takes longer and is considerably more expensive, or you can pay to have the bricks removed, which makes for a faster and less-expensive job.

You have two widely disparate views on the two types of jobs. Generally speaking, you can pay to have the bricks removed and then pay again, to have them put back. Or you can remove the bricks yourself and save a lot of money.

You can save even more by cleaning the bricks so that they can be used again, and thus save yourself the cost of buying the new bricks, unless you prefer another color or style.

If the house is covered with factory-red bricks that you detest, you can have them taken down and replaced by bricks more to your liking. If the mover's crew takes down the old bricks, you are paying them to do so. If you want to save the money involved, ask the mover if he will reduce his price if you take down the bricks.

Push your luck and ask him to show you how to do it. He can get you started and you can complete the job. Just be sure that he does not go off and start another job and leave you with a house that is getting soaked by rains and eaten by bugs.

If he agrees but does not have time to show you how to start, you can remove the bricks without trouble if you have a crowbar and a three-pound hammer. You will have to smash one brick, preferably on the corner, or even half a dozen, until you have broken the bond on the corner, at the top. When this is done, slip the blade of the crowbar or wrecking bar under the first bricks exposed to you and, if necessary, use the hammer to tap the end of the wrecking bar under the edge of the bricks.

Then pry outward, and you can hear the mortar joints breaking free of each other. You can pry out six or eight bricks at a time. You will be surprised just how weak a mortar joint is when exposed to stress from the side. When the weight or force is from the top, the bricks hold remarkably well, but they will not resist stress applied against the mortar joints.

**Figure 6-3**
*Using a mortar hammer to clean bricks.*

**Figure 6-4**
*Note how the mortar starts to separate from the brick.*

**Figure 6-5**
*Using a hammer and chisel to clean bricks.*

As you pry down bricks, haul them off as soon as you have a truckload. Bricks are heavy, as you know, and you should not try to haul more than 500 in a pickup truck bed. Even with that number you will find that your truck has remarkably easy power steering, even if it has no power steering at all. There will be so much weight on the rear axles and so little on the front end that you can steer easily. You can also just as easily have an accident.

If you must, you can pile the bricks in a heap at some point away from the work site. Use a wheelbarrow to haul them to the pile. And when you have the bricks removed, rent a truck if you have no other means of transportation. Or ask the mover to haul them in his truck.

If you don't have a wheelbarrow, you can afford to buy one with the money you saved, just as you can afford to rent a truck or hire someone to haul the bricks for you.

If you decide to clean the bricks, you can use a masonry hammer (which has a dull point on one end and a regular peen on the other) to tap the mortar loose. In most cases the mortar will fall off when you tap the dull point of the hammer at the point where the mortar has oozed over onto the top or bottom of the brick. See Figures 6-3 and 6-4. If the masonry hammer fails, you can buy a chisel and set the blade of the chisel into the point where mortar and brick meet and use a hammer to tap the chisel lightly. See Figure 6-5.

Incidentally, old bricks are worth money. In our part of the country salvage lumber and building-materials dealers pay ten cents apiece and up for used bricks. Some are worth far more.

Assuming that you plan to use the bricks in your house, pile the cleaned ones (as well as the halves and fourths) into neat stacks so that the full bricks can be counted easily. You will ruin some bricks, and you will need to buy some extras, so before you invest time and energy into the effort, be certain that you can locate and buy bricks that will be a perfect match for your own.

The last point is one that must be made, no matter which avenue you take on the moving job. If the old bricks are to be used, you may find that the aging process has caused the bricks to change color slightly but noticeably, and there will be a distinctive line where the old bricks stop and the new bricks start. This point is valid particularly if you leave the bricks on the house, except along the foundation walls, and the masons must re-brick this part of the house with new bricks.

If you need more bricks and can find only new ones that do not match perfectly, you can ask the masons to use the newer bricks where they will not show, such as on the back of the house or where shrubbery will conceal the slight discrepancies.

Let me remind you that the professional movers insist that there is very little difference in cost between moving a house with the bricks left on or taking down the bricks and then re-bricking the house. It's your choice.

The chimney or chimneys are also your choice. It is possible to move a house with the chimneys intact, but the move is more expensive than it is if you tear down the chimneys. The same basic principle of brick veneering holds true with chimneys. You can move it and pay more, or you can let the mover tear it down and rebuild it. The price is about the same either way, and the same holds true concerning the color of bricks and the faint difference between new and old bricks that do not match satisfactorily.

You can also compromise and tear down part of the chimney, the part that extends upward beyond the roof line. When you have the chimney rebuilt, there will still be a slight color problem that will last until the sun ages the new bricks and mortar, but this problem will be barely noticeable to anyone but you.

When we moved our house there was a brick mismatch that I could see even in the dark, and I felt obligated to explain the substandard work to people who came to see the house. But I found myself trying without success to get them to see the discrepancy. So I stopped trying, and now even I couldn't point out the problem.

As stated above, if you want to save money, you can take down the bricks and perhaps do the re-bricking job. Or, as I suggested in an earlier chapter, you can hire a mason and then you can work as his laborer or helper.

When the house is moved, you can salvage the cement blocks if you wish. Although many building codes will not permit you to use old blocks for load-bearing walls, such as foundation walls, you can use the blocks for a hundred types of projects or odd jobs around the house and garden.

In order to salvage blocks without breaking them (and cement blocks are surprisingly fragile), you will need to break the first block by striking it in the side with the three-pound hammer. When the block cracks, take it out of the wall and set the pieces aside.

Then, with the mortar cleared away from the unbroken block below the broken one, run the blade of the crowbar under the next block and, using the angle of the blade as a fulcrum, pry downward with slight pressure, increasing only as needed, until you hear and feel the mortar joint breaking. See Figure 6-6. You can then set the block out of the wall and proceed to the next block.

In each row of blocks, or course, you will need to break at least one block. But by working as described above, you can salvage hundreds of blocks which, if bought new, could cost you hundreds of dollars. Each block runs more than $1 each, so the effort is worth your time.

Part of the agreement in the house-moving deal may be that you must clean up the lot once the house is moved. If you or the mover must cut trees in order to move the house, you can use a chain saw to cut the trees into firewood length and then haul the wood home to use as fuel or sell it to someone who burns firewood. You can also chain-saw the trunk of the tree into great lumber that needs only planing to be highly valuable and beautiful.

If you are interested in chain-sawing, see my book entitled *How to Build Your Own Log Home for Under $15,000* (Loompanics Unlimited, 1996). There are chapters dealing with how to saw great lumber from trees. You can saw any dimension lumber from a 1 x 2 up to a 2 x 12 or larger, whatever the log will yield.

When you settle on a turnkey job, draw up an agreement that states specifically that the final payment is not due until the house has been rendered completely ready for occupancy. Do not ask the mover to trust you to meet your obligations, and in return he should not ask you to trust him to keep his word. This is strictly a business matter, even (or especially) if the mover is your brother-in-law.

Chapter Seven is concerned with some of the jobs that you must learn to do if you plan to do the necessary work yourself on a point-to-point job.

**Figure 6-6**
*Using a crowbar to pry blocks loose in foundation wall.*

# Chapter Seven
# Preparing for the Point-to-Point Move

You have, we shall assume, made the deal and also the decision to enter into the point-to-point agreement, and the mover has loaded the truck and is ready to start toward your property. Long before the truck gets there, there are several steps you can take that will make the delivery smoother, easier, and cheaper.

First, if there is a road leading into your property and to the house site, check the road carefully to ascertain that there is ample room for the house to move up the road without difficulty. If the road is hard-surfaced, so much the better. If it is not, you may need to check the route for potholes, washouts, and other problems that could create rough traveling for your new house.

Measure the width of the house. If it is 40-feet-wide, use a 100-foot measuring tape and check along the road to see if there is room between trees, well houses, and other natural or man-made obstructions for the house to pass with space to spare. Do not expect the driver to fit a 40-foot house into a 41-foot wide space. Trim back tree limbs that might damage the house by breaking window panes or scratching the siding.

If there are benches, picnic tables, or other yard niceties that are in the way, move these long before the truck with the house arrives. If the road has not been cut into the property, and if the house must travel over an open field, check the field for holes, large rocks, and stumps. If there are holes, fill these in. If there are stumps, either use a chain saw to cut the stump down to ground level or mark the stump clearly so that the truck driver will not run over it.

Select the exact location for the house. Decide where you will want the well, the septic tank, and the drain field. Be sure that the septic tank is downhill from the well and a safe distance from the drinking water. By "safe distance" I suggest at least a hundred feet or, preferably, more if you have a drilled well. If you have a bored well, I would want the septic tank as far from the well as I could have it and still keep the drain field on my own property, and always downhill. You can risk serious illness and even death by having contaminated drinking water.

It is good, if at all possible, to have the well drilled before the house arrives. There is always the chance that you will not hit water and will need to relocate the well site. Given a choice of a bored well, which is shallow as a rule, and a drilled well, I'd never hesitate to choose the drilled well.

The essential difference is that with a bored well you hit water before you strike rock tables. With a drilled well, you hit rock before you hit water, and the drill punches through the rock to the underground aquifers below.

The bored well is subject to contamination by surface water or other liquids and even solids that are deposited near the well opening. Gas, oil, and harmful chemicals can seep through the soil and enter the drinking water. A drilled well is as a rule very clean and pure, and you have a fairly good guarantee that you will always have an adequate good supply of water.

As an example, when our neighbors with bored wells found that their drinking water had dried up, we with our drilled well had almost a hundred feet of water remaining. When we had the state labs test our water, the report was astonishingly good, and the water has remained good to this day.

In many locations you can have a choice of county-wide water or well water. We opted for both. We used the county water for our garden and for washing cars, and we use the well for all of our bath and drinking water. And, only recently, county water levels became so low at the reservoir that hundreds of families in our area were without water while our supply was apparently unlimited.

When the site for the house has been chosen, mow the grass and weeds where the house will sit, and then mow farther back so that there will be plenty of open space for the workers. You do not want them wading through underbrush and risking stings by bees and other insect pests, chiggers, ticks, and even snake bites. These encounters can result in delays in getting your house ready.

Mark off the area where the house will be located. Use stakes and cords to mark the entire house area. It does not have to be totally square or precisely accurate. You are simply giving the driver the best indication you can of where the house is to be located.

At this point your work is temporarily done. You must wait until the house is in place, and then you can take care of the problem of the footings.

It would be nice if you could dig and pour the footings before the house arrived, because once the house is in place you must dig under the sills, which is rather difficult until the trench is deep enough to let you stand while you work.

However, because you don't know exactly where the house will sit or whether the house is perfectly square, you cannot dig the trenches and expect the house to sit perfectly over the footings. So, with the house in place, you start to work, or you hire someone to do the work for you.

Because this is a book about how to save a great deal of money — literally thousands and thousands of dollars — I will assume that you prefer to do as much of the work as you can. If you hire everything done, your savings will be cut severely.

When you start to dig the trenches for the footings, you must drop a perpendicular line from the center of the sill to the ground, or you can use a five-foot length of 2 x 4 or similar timber against the side of the house so that one end of the piece of timber rests on the soil beneath the sills and the other end is positioned against the siding of the house.

Now hold a level against the timber. Be certain that the timber is perfectly vertical. When it is, mark with a mattock or hoe where the bottom end of the timber rests. Mark several places along the wall, and when you have done this, start to dig. There are ditching machines that will do the work for you quickly and rather inexpensively; however, it is impossible to get the ditcher into position. Sadly, the work must be done manually.

The tools you will need are a mattock or pick — or both — and a shovel. Use the mattock or pick to loosen the dirt under the sills and then use the shovel to scoop up the loose dirt and toss it away from the trench.

At this point you need to understand that a footing trench is a ditch that is about eight inches wider than the sill of the house. The sill is the flat board, usually a 2 x 8, that the joists are nailed to.

The sill, in a sense, supports the entire perimeter weight of the house.

**Figure 7-1**
*Dumping gravel under the porch roof for handy access.*

**Figure 7-2**
*Dumping part of the gravel outside the wall for use in other work areas.*

**Figure 7-3**
*Removing damaged sills.*

Actually the foundation wall supports the weight, but the sill sits on the foundation wall, and the joists sit on the sill. The studs and wall framing generally sit on the joists, and the eaves of the roof sit on the wall frames. So you can see that the foundation walls are extremely important. If the foundation walls should crumble and collapse, the entire wall of the house would do likewise.

Similarly, if the foundation wall sinks five or six inches on one end — or on both ends — the wall must sink also, and soon the rooms are out of square, the floors are not level, there are huge cracks along floor and ceiling lines, and the brick veneer, if any, will crack and admit cold or hot air, insects, and moisture into the house. The house becomes totally unsatisfactory when there is such extreme sinking, or settling.

The way to prevent the settling is to dig trenches that are deep enough that the bottom of the trench is below the frost or freeze line. In some states, that point is barely beneath the surface of the ground. In others, it is easily two feet or much deeper.

Why the emphasis on the freeze or frost line? At a depth where there is a freezing temperature, the moisture in the earth freezes and the frozen water and soil holding the moisture will expand, buck, and exert great pressure outward. This pressure will disrupt the footings, and when the ice thaws the house will sink where the footings were disturbed.

Dig your footings trench, then, below the frost line. That may be two feet or more. And be certain to dig below the layer of topsoil that is too soft to support the footing. Some parts of the country have little or no topsoil, while others have several inches. To be safe, stick to the two-foot suggestion, or 18 inches at least.

Our method of pouring footings was, after we had dug the trenches, to have our gravel, sand, bags of mortar, and mixing equipment as handy to the work as possible. We built a ramp so that when the gravel was delivered, it could be dumped under the porch, as shown in Figure 7-1. Because we would need gravel on the outside of the covered areas as well, we had the truck positioned so that at least half of the gravel would be outside the basic wall we constructed to outline the porch area. See Figure 7-2.

This is a good time to check for damaged timbers, as we are doing in Figure 7-3. We had sills that were damaged, and we took these out before we went any further with our work. Later, we replaced them.

When you are ready to begin, dig along the entire length of the first wall. When you reach the corner, be sure you dig a few extra inches to permit the concrete to settle deep enough at the corners. Now dig along the next line, and keep up the work until you have dug around the entire wall. Remember that your footing trench should be wider than your wall sills.

If you plan to add brick veneer to the walls, you must have four inches of concrete for the bottom bricks to rest upon. And you will need a little extra room, because you do not want the bricks to rest at the very edge of the concrete. So allow at least six inches for the bricks.

When the ditch is completed, you need to dump two inches of sand into the ditch and spread it to a uniform length along the entire ditch. Then add two inches of coarse gravel.

When this is done, mix your concrete and pour the finished product on top of the gravel until you have a footing that is the required depth for your part of the country.

If you do not know the proper depth, ask the building inspector. Incidentally, you may have to permit the inspector to come out to examine your footing trench before you pour concrete or lay any blocks.

Some areas do not require an inspection for houses that have been moved. Don't take chances. Call and ask. Remember that the building inspector is not your enemy. His job is to see that you do not build a dwelling that will be unsafe for you and your family.

When you mix concrete, you can do it by hand, but this is hard and time-consuming. It is much easier to rent a portable mixer and use it. The mixer can do the work while you handle other chores, and it can last longer than your back can. In Figure 7-4 my wife Elizabeth is operating the mixer while I work on the footings.

Ask your dealer for the cement about the best mixture for your area, or read the directions on the cement bags. Many think that a 1-3-5 mixture of cement, sand, and gravel is good, with enough water to create a plastic but not watery mixture. The sand is termed the fine aggregate, and the gravel is referred to as the coarse aggregate.

In the mixture the powdery cement will coat the granules of sand, and the sand and cement combination will coat the gravel, giving you a mixture that will hold together under virtually all types of stress and climates.

You must have the cement or concrete level in the trench. If you do not, your foundation wall will be uneven.

How do you get the footing level? The easy and cheap way is to do it with stakes driven into the ground in the bottom of the trench. You'll need enough stakes to drive one every two feet or so. At each end of the trench drive a stake and then tie one end of the line-level cord to each of those end stakes.

A line level is, as the term implies, a small instrument about four inches long that can be hooked or snapped onto a small cord. The level itself has a plastic cylinder marked with lines across it. Inside the cylinder there is a liquid with a bubble inside it. When the instrument is held so that the bubble is exactly between the lines, the instrument is level.

Tie the ends of the cord to the end stakes, and then hang the level about the middle of the cord. Check it for accuracy. If the bubble is not centered, raise or lower one end of the cord until you get a perfect reading.

With the cord pulled taut and tied, work along the cord and drive stakes into the ground so that the top of each stake is perfectly even with the cord. When you pour concrete, let the level of the top of the concrete be even with the top of the stake. Remove the cord before pouring concrete.

Stretch the line level and drive stakes along all four walls. Be sure that the second wall line is level with the line of the first wall line. When this is done, you are ready to pour the concrete.

Earlier it was suggested that you might want to mix and pour your own. You can also buy ready-mixed concrete, and when the truck arrives the driver will pour the footings in a matter of minutes. If you do it yourself, it will take days, perhaps a week.

The decision is one you must make in terms of money and time. Can you afford the cost of having the concrete poured? Can you afford the time it will take you to pour it yourself? You are the only one who can answer those questions.

At this point you need to think about the foundation walls as well. And about a basement.

Do you want a basement in your new house? If so, you need to talk with someone who can dig the basement for you. A front-end loader will do the work in a short time, three or four hours, while it will take you days and days of grueling labor to accomplish the same by manual labor.

If you plan to have a basement, have it dug while the house is in its early stages. You can do

**Figure 7-4**
*Operating the portable mixer.*

as we did and have a double wall in the basement, or you can let the foundation wall for the house also act as the basement wall. Obviously I preferred the double wall for several reasons, among them strength, insulation, and utility.

Because you are going to be working with concrete and mortar for a while, it is wise to have the dealer deliver truckloads of sand, gravel, and bags of mortar mix or cement. Have these placed near the house but not in the way of the truck that will haul the house to the site. Be sure that the bags of cement are protected from the weather. And under-order if possible. Many dealers will not accept returned mixes because so many people let the bags get wet and the mix hardens until it cannot be used.

When the house is delivered, it will remain on the steel until you have the foundation wall ready and the house can be lowered onto the wall. Chapter Eight discusses, among other things, building the foundation wall and pouring the basement floor, in the event you choose to include one.

# Chapter Eight
# Basement Floors and
# Foundation Walls

If you want a basement, now is the time to pour the concrete floor. You will need to scoop out dirt, rocks, and debris until you have a nearly level surface. And you will use the same pattern of sand, gravel, and concrete that you used earlier.

The big difference makes a mighty difference in the end. After you put in the layer of sand and the layer of gravel, you will need to spread a layer of plastic or polyethylene over the gravel. Then you will pour the concrete over the plastic.

The purpose of the plastic is to act as a moisture barrier so that dampness will not seep upward through the concrete. Take care that you do not punch holes in the plastic as you work. Even the smallest holes will admit an incredible amount of water into the basement.

Before you start to pour the concrete floor, you need to pour the footings for the basement walls. We can assume that if you poured footings for the perimeter of the house, you are ready to lay the foundation walls and then pour the basement concrete.

You need not build the entire foundation wall if you have to work on the basement quickly. There are reasons, at times, for the haste. Perhaps you have the opportunity to avail yourself of a portable mixer, or you may have friends who are willing to help you with the work. The rainy season may be near and you may need to get the work done before the heavy rains flood the basement area.

Assume that your basement is 1,600 square feet. This is a lot of concrete to pour in one day, unless you have the ready-mix materials delivered to your house. In that event, you should have all the forms constructed so that when the concrete arrives it can be poured within seconds. Do not have the driver wait while you complete work that should have been done before you even called the concrete supply company.

Decide how much work you plan to do in one day. The ready-mix approach is fast, and you should be able to pour the entire basement in one day. However, if you choose to mix and pour your own concrete, work out an installment manner of work.

One workable plan is to lay out the basement with stakes, just as you did the footings, and to level the stake tops with a line level. If you prefer, when one stake is ready, you can use a timber, such as a 2 x 4, with a straight edge across the stakes. Place a level on the top edge of the 2 x 4, and then drive down any stakes that are higher than the bottom edge of the 2 x 4 when it is in a horizontal and level position.

Another workable plan is to lay out the basement rooms, if you plan to divide it, and pour the concrete for one room at a time. The reason for this is that wherever you stop for the day and start back the next day, there will be a clearly visible line that will show no matter how carefully your pour and smooth.

If you know that, for instance, in the back of the basement there will be a furnace room that will be 12′ by 12′, you can use boards to lay out the room and you can pour that entire room in one work session. Later, when the dividing walls are erected, the seam will be concealed by the wall.

To use boards as forms to lay out a wall, you will need boards that are six inches wide. Two inches of that width will be accounted for by the sand; another two inches will be taken up by the gravel or coarse aggregate; and the final two inches will be used by the concrete.

Don't be concerned by the apparent thinness of the layer of concrete. Two inches of concrete will support an incredible weight. An engineer once told me that a two-inch concrete slab would be adequate for the floor of a garage that will hold full-sized cars and trucks.

Stand the boards on edge after you have nailed 12″ stakes to the outside of the board. There should be a stake at each end of the board and at least one near the center. When you stand the board on edge, drive the stakes into the ground so that the board is well-supported. Lay out all four wall areas so that you have a 12-foot square bounded by boards six inches high. Be sure that the tops of the boards are all level.

Now dump in the sand and gravel, and then cover it with plastic before you pour the concrete. Next, mix concrete and haul it in a wheelbarrow to the area. Dump the concrete and return to mix more, while your helper uses a flat smoothing device with which to pat and rub the concrete to push all the gravel edges under the surface and to pull the watery fluid to the top. You can smooth the fluid with easy, gentle, circular movements.

From time to time lay a 12-foot board on edge across the room area and check to see if the concrete is higher than the bottom edge of the board. If it is, the concrete needs to be worked down or some of it should be scooped out.

You can even get someone on each end of the board and the two of you can work the board, held erect, across the concrete to sweep or bulldoze the excess concrete to the edge where it can be removed. When you have finished with the 12-foot room area, let the concrete dry overnight before you walk on it. In fact, it is better to allow two or three days, if you can.

Concrete, unlike many dense substances, does not dry or set up quickly. Engineers tell us that concrete will continue to set or harden for decades after it is poured.

When the first section is completed, set up forms for the next section, and continue in this manner until the entire basement floor is poured. The foundation walls will provide the forms for one or two of the sides of the forms, so you will have to set up only two or three for each room.

If you plan to leave a large expanse of basement floor open, you will need to plan to work hard for as long as you can, or until the work is done. Plan to devote the entire day to the work, and rise early and get the earliest start you can. Have all of the materials ready to go the previous day, so that when you reach the work site all you need to do is crank up the mixer and start working.

Don't plan for long lunches or early stops that day. Plan to stay on the job until it is completed or until you reach the best of all possible stopping points.

When you begin work on the foundation walls, one of the jobs you will want to complete early is that of waterproofing the exterior side of the walls. You can buy any of several brands of sealers, and these can be applied with brushes or with trowels, depending upon the type of sealer used. Start at the lowest point you can reach and apply the sealer as thickly as you can. If necessary, apply a second coating after the first has dried.

Keep rising with the sealer until you have completely covered the wall from the footing to the highest blocks that will be fully or partially underground. There is no need to seal the blocks that will be above ground.

One of the earliest jobs after the sealer has been applied is that of buying and installing drain tiles. These come in lengths of eight feet (some perhaps longer) and you can get bends or right-angle sections. You will need to lay the tiles so that the highest point is the farthest point from the drain area. Let the tiles slant downward only slightly from the high point to the low point.

When the drain tiles are installed and connected, cover them with large or coarse gravel. Use at least six inches of gravel on top of the tiles. You can backfill later with dirt.

The purpose of the drain tiles is to allow moisture from the ground and from run-off from rains to sink into the soil and then permeate the tiles by seeping through the holes in the tops and sides. Then the water will flow to the exit areas and away from the house.

A wet basement is a continuing source of irritation and problems. A dry basement is a wonderful part of the house. Do not be fooled into thinking that it is easy to keep the basement dry. Some houses remain wet underneath during their entire existence. Wet basements will cause rot, attract termites, and encourage mildew. Anything stored in the basement is likely to be damaged within a matter of days.

When your outside basement walls are sealed and the drain tile is in place, turn your attention to the inside walls. Here you can use a clear sealer that will not mar or discolor the walls. Apply the sealer with a brush or roller. Use plenty of sealer, and then let the first coat dry. Then add another. You may want to use as many as three coats.

You can also buy sealer that can be used in a sprayer. Even a garden sprayer will work well. Spray the entire wall, and then spray heavily at the seam where the foundation wall and the basement floor meet. Let the sealer dry and then spray again.

You may also want to parget your basement walls, inside and out. When you parget (pronounced par-zhay) a wall, you actually apply a form of stucco. You mix mortar and then use the back of the trowel to scoop up mortar and smear it on the wall. Use an upward arcing motion, and spread the mortar on as evenly as you can.

The next trowel-load should lap over the first load slightly. Pause to scrape the surface into the neatest and smoothest possible manner. When you are finished, the wall will have a stucco look, and you will have helped to seal it even more.

Later, if you choose, you can affix rocks on the wall if you want the stone look. Obviously the rock will be only on that part of the wall that rises higher than the soil around the house.

You can enlist the aid of a professional mason to complete the foundation walls, or, if you can follow instructions and use meticulous care, you can lay the walls yourself. Consult a good reference book for the best methods of mixing mortar, or use a 1-3 mixture of mortar mix and sand. Use enough water to create a plastic mix that will hold its shape loosely when you pile it on a mortar board. You do not want the mixture to be so thin that it runs, or so thick that it crumbles.

Your most important considerations when you are building the foundation walls are to keep the walls level and even as they rise and to be certain that the finished wall will rise exactly under the sills of the house. To keep the walls level, start at the corners and lay the first corner block. Then butt the next block against the side of the first block. Go to the next corner and do the same thing. Keep on moving until you have laid all four corners.

Then stretch a line from the top edge of the first corner block to the first block of the next corner. Now stretch another block line to the next corner. Start laying blocks in one corner, and be certain that all block tops are level with the block tops at the adjacent corner.

**Figure 8-1**
*Laying a foundation wall under the house resting on steel.*

**Figure 8-2**
*Trimming timbers to use under the hydraulic jack.*

Build all four corners all the way to the top. Then lay the blocks between the corner blocks until the entire wall is at the same height and even all around. Figure 8-1 shows the process of laying foundation wall blocks under the house, which was left by the mover on the timbers. Note that the steel which really supports the house is resting on cross-stacked oak timbers. The house will rest on the steel until the foundation walls are nearly complete.

I say "nearly complete" because you cannot finish the wall if the steel remains in place. Lay the wall as high as you can, but leave out the blocks for the section directly under the steel. When the steel is pulled out, it will destroy the part of the wall under it, so omit that part until the final stages.

If the house needs adjustment in height, you can use a small hydraulic jack to lift a corner of the house to the desired level. To use the hydraulic jack (which can be purchased for a very small amount of money, or perhaps you can use one of the jacks belonging to the mover), shovel out the loose dirt under the jack and then locate solid concrete blocks or thick sections of timbers. If you must use timber sections, be sure the sections are straight and flat. Lay these flat upon the space you have cleared and then set the jack on top of the timbers. Cut the timber sections, as shown in Figure 8-2, to meet your needs.

Use the jack screw to tighten the fit under the steel, and when the jack is ready, begin to pump the jack slowly and evenly until the house is raised the inch or two necessary for the work you are doing. Figure 8-3 shows the process of slowly jacking up the house.

Do not leave the house weight resting upon the jack, which is too easy to dislodge. Instead, stack timbers under the steel, or build permanent piers to support the house at several key positions.

When the walls that can be completed have been finished, you can lower the house onto the steel by jacking the house up slightly as you did before and then using pry bars, as shown in Figure 8-4, to shift the steel so that the timbers can be taken from under it. Then the steel can be removed from under the house.

When the house has been lowered onto the foundation wall, you can slide the timbers, as shown in Figure 8-5, from under the house. Stack these in a safe place so that the mover can pick them up when he returns for his steel. These 6 x 8 or larger timbers are of oak and are very strong and durable, but they are also expensive, and the mover will assuredly need them for later work.

You can now complete any remaining work on the wall. There is one major difference between building a foundation wall under a house and building one upon which the house will be built. You need to have the blocks come out exactly right; that is, the top of the final course of foundation wall blocks should be about

four inches below the bottom of the house sills. You can lay cap blocks here, if you wish. Normally you would want to have anchor bolts

**Figure 8-3**
*Jacking up the house slightly to complete foundation walls.*

**Figure 8-4**
*Prying the steel free to remove it.*

installed in the top course of blocks, but you will have a difficult time installing the anchor bolts, since the sills are several inches above the blocks and you cannot work out the spacing and setting of the anchor bolts as you normally would.

**Figure 8-5**
*Taking out the support timbers.*

Here are two methods that will work. First, drill a hole for the anchor bolt up through the bottom of the sill. Make sure that the bolt will sink into a cavity in the block as the house is lowered. Run the end of the anchor bolt up through the hole in the sill, and then put a washer and nut on the end of the bolt. Let the bolt hang from the sill for the present.

When all of the anchor bolts have been installed in this manner, you can use a trowel to fill the top blocks with mortar or concrete. Then, when the mover lowers the house to its final position, the ends of the bolts will sink into the cavities in the blocks and into the mortar.

If you have trouble working the anchor bolts into the sill hole, you might want to try buying threaded rods and cutting the rods to the length of anchor bolts. At what will be the bottom of

the anchor bolt install a large washer and a bolt below the washer. Lower the bolt into the cavity until the top end clears the edge of the block, and then push the top end up through the hole in the sill. Now add a washer and nut to the top of the bolt, and then you can lower the bolts into the mortar-filled cavities in the blocks.

Check with the building inspector concerning how far apart the anchor bolts should be. It's slightly more costly to do it this way, but I prefer to have an anchor bolt in every block, or about every two feet.

Here is a third way to install my personal version of the anchor bolt. This method is to me far better than any of the other methods, and these home-made bolts hold enormously well and offer far more security. My method is to bolt a length of 2 x 4 to the joists so that the 2 x 4 is fitted snugly against the foundation wall, with the four-inch edge against the wall. Do this every two feet. Let the 2 x 4s reach to the bottom of the foundation wall if you can afford the treated lumber.

Then drill a hole through the edge of the 2 x 4 and use a masonry bit to drill a hole through the block itself. Now push a threaded rod through the 2 x 4 and through the cement block. You will need to add a washer and a nut on the outside of the wall and another on the inside.

Now the house foundation wall is bolted to the 2 x 4 which in turn is bolted to the joists. From then on, any wind strong enough to rip the 2 x 4s loose from the foundation wall is also strong enough to tear the house apart.

You can use the 2 x 4s for the addition of interior walls. You can fasten panels of plywood or other wall covering, and you will have a finished look to your basement.

When the wall has been completed and after the mortar joints have dried and set up, you can call the mover and he will return and lower the house to the foundation walls, if you have not done so. If there is any doubt about the work, let the mover do it. He is the professional. And if there is a problem, let it be his, not yours. The mover will be very slow and gentle as he lowers the house to the foundation wall.

If you wish to do as we did, you can build your interior basement walls three feet inside the foundation walls. As noted earlier, you can let the three feet of dead air space act as insulation, or, again like us, you can use the area for storage space for potatoes and other crops that keep well in a cool type of environment.

Laying blocks is a skill that anyone can master, as long as all you are doing is, as one mason puts it, "stacking blocks." I do not mean to imply that it is easy in every sense, but it is a skill that can be learned in a short time. My wife, who is shown completing a section of wall in Figure 8-6, and I had never laid a block in our lives, and yet we completed the foundation walls of the house, poured the basement floor, and built the basement walls without trouble. A professional mason might well laugh at our efforts, but he will not laugh all the way to the bank — with our money.

At this point the walls and the basement floor are completed, and the mover can remove his timbers and steel and leave you to the remainder of the job.

Chapter Nine deals with the restoration of some of the outside or peripheral parts of the house that you had to take down so that you could move the house.

**Figure 8-6**
*Completing the basement walls.*

# Chapter Nine
# Handling Outbuildings
## and Extensions

In an age when nearly every family in the small town owns at least one automobile or truck, riding mowers, and other items designed to make life easier or more enjoyable, one of the common requirements of these items of comfort is some place to keep them. This means that storage buildings, garages, car ports, and other outside storage areas have been added to the typical house.

Other items you will notice if you move an older house are the side porch, front porch, and back porch. Often these building additions and extensions were added as an afterthought, long after the house was completed.

Your problem of how to deal with these outbuildings or the extensions of the house proper can be easily handled. As far as large porches are concerned, these comfort areas were often built as part of the house, and the roof of the main house extends to cover the porch. So it is difficult to disregard the porch and consign it to the landfill.

The financial aspect of the carport, garage, or porch is also an important part of the consider-ation. Adding a garage can easily cost as much as an entire house cost a few years ago. You can figure that your garage is worth $5,000, or even several times that amount. A porch adds comfort to the house and also to the value of your house once it has been restored. Look at Figure 9-1 and then imagine the house without the porch. A huge amount of the financial worth and almost half the aesthetic value of the house would be lost without the porch.

The house in Figure 9-2 has several porches, all of which can be moved along with the house. Your cost would not increase greatly. Such porches are relatively easy to move. Even a small porch such as the one in Figure 9-3 adds greatly to the appearance of the house.

In Figure 9-4 you can see the old-fashioned "country" porch, which served a multitude of purposes. In rainy weather the porch is large enough to offer a recreational area or outdoor play room; in hot weather the porch is a perfect place to sit and relax, or it is a work area for stringing beans, shucking corn, or peeling peaches for canning or freezing. At night in the hot months it is a naturally air-conditioned comfort area. Because it is screened-in, it is safe from bees, mosquitoes, and other pests, and is also protected from dogs, snakes, and other animals that may be pesky or dangerous.

The porch is a perfect playpen for the youngsters, and it can be used for picnics or for a dining area for large groups of people. We even used it as an extra sleeping area for company, particularly young ones who didn't mind a sleeping bag and a hard floor. And, if the need ever arises, the porch could be closed in and converted into a spare room. It did not cost an extra cent to move the porch area. The only expense was that of the flooring and screen wire.

**Figure 9-1**
*A long porch like this offers protection from weather.*

**Figure 9-2**
*A series of smaller porches add character to a house.*

There are two fairly easy ways to move the porches, even the side porches, if they were constructed as part of the main house. One way is simply to move the entire porch, just as if it were an extra room. If it is a front porch, the move is sometimes not very complicated, and even if it is a side porch, unless the porch makes the house too wide for the most economical move, the porch can be transported along with the house.

In Figure 9-5 you can see a front stoop that was left intact and a side porch that was also moved with the house. Notice the braces that supported the porch during the trip. The braces will be left in place until the foundation walls and floors are added to the house and the posts can be again put in place. In Figure 9-6 you can also see that some of the lower siding has been removed to prevent damage to it during transit.

Figure 9-7 shows the same house after it is nearly completely restored. Notice how the porches contribute greatly to the over-all appearance of the house. The wrought-iron support posts and railings also add to the appearance.

Fortunately, the side porch is often built onto the house and the roof of the side porch is simply attached to the side of the house. The main roof does not cover the side porch.

**Figure 9-3**
*Even a small porch contributes a note of charm to a house.*

**Figure 9-4**
*A porch of this type is an all-purpose addition to a house.*

**Figure 9-5**
*Side porches like this can be moved easily with the house.*

In such cases, if the porch must come down, the simple solution is to dismantle the porch, starting with the roof, and take down the shingles, rafters, ridge beam, and finally the posts. You can also take down the floor and foundation walls, if any.

Before you take down the porch, measure all of the basic dimensions and write down the measurements. Later you will want to restore the house to its original size and shape.

These materials can be hauled in a pickup truck, unless the porch is unusually large. The shingles should be discarded, since they will not be used a second time. The sheathing (sheeting) that covers the porch roof can be saved and used when the porch is put back up.

When the house is moved and you are finished with the work of foundation walls and basements, you can add the porch back to the house. Refer to your measurements and dig footings and pour these as you did before. Then add the foundation-wall blocks. The building inspector probably will permit you to use any blocks from the porch, since the blocks are not load-bearing wall units.

Lay the blocks as you did for the basement, except that now the work is much faster and easier. When the foundation wall is completed, add the sills and joists. You can probably use the ones you took down. The measurements should be exactly the same as the new porch you are adding, so no cutting is necessary.

When the joists are installed, nail in the sub-flooring and the flooring. Then install the support posts for the roof.

**Figure 9-6**
*The small front stoop offers no problems and adds to the looks of the house.*

**Figure 9-7**
*The nearly restored house is a great bargain for the cost.*

While the posts are unsupported and while they are not holding any weight, this is the time to be certain that you get a level reading on all of them. You can drive a stake in the yard, about five or six feet from the porch, and then you can hold the post erect while someone else nails the post to the brace piece which runs from post to stake and acts as a support for the post.

Do this for all four posts. Then nail up the cross members which run from one post to another. Cut a small length of 2 x 4 and nail it to the center of the cross member that runs at right angles to the ridge beam. Rest the bottom edge of the ridge beam on the top of the upright which rests on the cross member. Do this at the front and back of the porch roof line.

Now add the rafters. When this is done, nail up the roof sheathing. You are now ready to add the shingles to waterproof the roof of the porch.

If the floor of the porch is only a concrete slab not connected to the house, and if the porch does not make the house too wide for the trip, you can run strong support braces from the outer edge of the porch to the bottom of the house. Use one strong brace on each side of the porch. These cross braces will support the roof as the house makes its journey to the new site.

Here I am writing about a small side porch, not a porch large enough to allow eight or ten people to sit on it. If the porch is large, it should be taken down as described above.

Sometimes the floor of the front or back porch is the slab of concrete mentioned earlier. If this is the case, you cannot move the porch as part of the house without some strong support timbers.

If you must leave the floor part of the porch, you will need to use extra-heavy and strong support brace pieces. For this work I recommend 4 x 4 timbers, one placed where a post has been in place before. Again, run the brace pieces at an angle from the top of the porch frame to the bottom of the front or back walls of the house. The porch should ride safely in this fashion.

If there is a connected garage, chances are good that the garage cannot remain intact. It must be taken down, unless, of course, you are going to move the house for only a short trip, such as across the street or to the back of the lot.

Often the garage will not be framed into the house. That is, you will be able to take it down, much as you did the small porch, and leave the house intact. The framing timbers for the house do not extend to the garage, and the roofing members for the garage are separate from those in the house.

However, if you cannot separate the two building units cleanly, you will need to take the garage down, piece by piece, and when you come to the framing timbers you will simply cut them with a chain saw. As with all work of this sort, you need to take care not to break timbers or ruin their ends. A timber that is four inches too short is unsuited for the job, and you will need to buy new ones.

Remember that the garage or porch timbers were cut to fit inside a particular space. If you carelessly break one or if one of the crew members grabs up a garage timber and cuts off a chunk to use in another job, you will be minus that timber when it is time to complete the garage work.

Load the timbers into a pickup truck, and when you get them to the new house site, set them apart. And don't just dump them on the ground. Put down some scrap wood or similar materials that will keep the garage timbers off the ground. You may not get back to work on the garage for months, and people who work with wood know that only a few days in contact with wet ground can ruin good wood.

When I say to set the timbers apart, I mean to take them far enough from the house that they will not be picked up to use as a brace piece or other temporary solution to a minor carpentry job problem. If the garage is free-standing, the mover might be able to come back and move it intact. While this may cost you a little more, it is money well spent to have the garage moved as a whole.

By all means, do work such as disassembling the garage and porch by yourself. Do not pay a carpenter to pull nails. Pay him to do the work you cannot do. It is false economy to pay a man $20 to salvage a $12 timber.

As you take down timbers, pull the nails as soon as you can and collect them in a large metal bucket or similar container. I do not advocate cheapness to the miserly extent, but I heartily recommend rusty or used nails for carpentry work.

A nail is essentially a length of wire. When it is new it is shiny and slick, and when it is driven into wood its holding power comes from the fact that the nail shoves the wood fibers apart as far as it can, and the fibers naturally tend to resist movement, and therefore the tightness holds the nail in place. If the wood is slightly green when the nails are driven, as the wood dries the nails loosen. This is one of the reasons you see so many warped boards with loose ends in old (and sometimes new) buildings.

But a rusty nail is rough, and it clings to wood fibers better than a new nail will, and while you save some money on nails, your real reward lies in the greater holding power.

When you start to re-assemble the garage, if you notice that the ends of rafters and other timbers have started to soften or rot, do not use the timbers. Do not use boards that have also lost their integrity. You will be taking the boards or timbers down in the near future to replace them.

What you can do, in many cases, is cut off the bad ends and use the timbers or boards in other areas. Often only the end is bad, and it rotted because there was a leak or condensation where it was nailed to the framing of the building.

If possible, keep the wood covered while you are waiting for time to get back to the job. When raindrops or dew settle on a piece of wood, and then the sun shines through the drops of water, there is a magnified heat build-up, and the paint on the wood begins to bubble and flake. If the

wood is not painted, there will be a speedy deterioration.

If you question this observation, notice how many buildings have flaking paint and rot on the east side. This deterioration is caused partially by the dew moisture that clings to the wood in the early morning. The sun then shines through the droplets and does the damage. Why no greater damage on the west? The dew is dried from the heat of the day long before the sun shines on the west side of the building.

One consideration not mentioned up to this point is that of liability. When you leave timbers lying around, it is only a matter of time before some worker steps on a rusty nail and needs medical attention. You can bet that neighborhood children — and even adults — will want to come over and watch the progress of your work, and if one of them is injured, you may face a legal action.

Don't take chances. Keep the work area clean and safe.

For your own safety, wear protective gloves anytime you are working with wood and other building materials. Be alert for bees and other stinging and biting insects. Wear protective glasses at all times, and wear the hard hats seen at construction sites. Wear long sleeves and pants. Bare arms and legs are invitations to injuries or skin irritations. When you are taking walls apart, remember that there might be raccoons, rats, snakes, and other animal pests nesting in the area.

Even when the area is uninhabited by animals, wear the protective gear. Animal waste left behind can cause disease and serious health problems. Remember that squirrels can inflict very painful bites, and these furry little creatures can be highly aggressive when provoked. The opossum is equipped with long, sharp teeth which can penetrate completely through a man's hand.

Many of these animals carry rabies. Scientifically, all warm-blooded animals can carry rabies, and raccoons and foxes and dogs are highly susceptible. The possum, for reasons that are unclear, seems to resist rabies infection better than do cats, dogs, bats, foxes, and coons.

These creatures also leave spores and parasites where they have lived, and the human being can pick up several diseases from the animal parasites. There is a possibility of ringworm, fleas, lice, and other annoying health problems.

One matter that will arise in many house-moving projects is that of the basement that is left behind. Do not simply haul off the house and leave an open hole 40 feet long, 24 feet wide, and nine feet deep. If it is a cellar type of basement, the hole may contain water after heavy rains, and neighborhood children and pets may be in danger, as is anyone who stumbles and falls into the hole. So make arrangements with the mover to use his earth-moving equipment to fill the basement.

To close on an optimistic note after a series of warnings, these cautions are only that: it would be remiss of me not to mention these potential problems. But house moving is almost invariably a win-win situation.

Unless there are catastrophic events, such as natural disasters, wrecks, fires, or the like — and these are potentially there in nearly all of our endeavors — you are not likely to encounter any serious difficulties. Oh, to be sure, there will be problems, just as there are when you decide to modify the door frame or light switch, but from a pragmatic standpoint, you will not only be able to deal with the challenges but overcome them.

When the move is over and the house is set up for occupancy, you will be able to sit down and start counting assets and a few liabilities. You will realize that you spent, counting your outlay for land, cost of moving, repairs, permits, and other expenses, as much as $20,000 — or as little as $10,000.

But what did you get in return? In many cases, you received a house worth $150,000 or far more. Even if you count your labor time as an expense, you will be handsomely compensated for your work. You will probably realize that

you could not have earned as much money in any job you are capable of holding as you did when you chose to embark on the house-moving adventure.

And, to make the bottom line better, in Chapter 10 you will learn that if you decide to make a few improvements while you are in the work mode, you can add thousands and thousands of dollars to the value of your home. You may decide that while the equipment is handy, you might as well make progress on some of the additions to the house you would likely make in the future. I predict that you will be pleasantly amazed at the way the value of your house soars with only modest additions.

# Chapter Ten
# Making a Great Bargain Better

When the move is completed and the house is essentially ready for you to move into, this is a superb time to make the last-second improvements that you'd planned to make later, after you were settled in your nearly new house. Like most good intentions, this one will be relegated to its place in a dark closet.

Said another way, this is the best possible time to make the improvements, and if you don't do the jobs now, the chances are good that you never will. At this point you have not settled into the house, and you are tired, your money is running low, and you want to move into your house and rest.

Before you make that decision, look at facts and figures relative to home improvements. You may be awed by the cost of these improvements, particularly in light of the bargain you have just received.

What follows is intended to be an example of what you can do with a house that had to be modified before it could be moved. This is not intended to be a house-construction book, and there will not be intricate detail offered; however, the following material is essentially what you will need to accomplish if you should decide to follow up on the opportunity to make your house even more valuable.

And, because the material is general, it can be used in any number of other circumstances. The basic plan suggested here could be utilized in case you wish to add a spare bedroom, a den, or family room. The work detailed here begins at a point when the joists are already in place.

You may find the material useful, because too often home owners who decided to convert their one-story house to a two-story residence will pay an average price of more than $45,000 for the completed project — more by far than you paid for your entire house and costs of moving and restoration. But what if you find a great house to move, except that it's too high for the many wires stretched along the route and the only way it can be moved it by taking off the roof and roof framing? By doing so you can get the house for nothing or nearly nothing.

You would not normally consider such an endeavor, but you need a house badly, particularly a cheap house, and the only one available is the one with the too-high roof. Or suppose that you happen to like that particular house well enough to invest the money and time in moving it.

Now carry the supposition one step further. The house, which you can buy for $100 and move for $7,000, will be worth about $95,000 when the move is completed. Now, if you decide to make the house a two-story dwelling, your finished product is now worth $150,000 or slightly more.

But you can't afford the cost of adding a floor to the house. So you give up the opportunity to increase the value of your house.

Now look at it another way. If you hired someone to add a second story to your house, you'd pay the crew first to remove the roof of your house and then take down all the roof framing, including rafters, collar bracing, and all the rest.

But you just paid someone to take down these timbers! That part of the job is free, relative to the second story. Now all you have to do is pay to have the second story built.

Still too much money? Not if you are willing to do much of the work yourself. But you have no idea where to begin, so you put the dream behind you.

**Figure 10-1**
*The house with only the top part of the roof removed.*

But why not make the dream come true? One of the great bargains in housing is the second story. You know, of course, that one roof can cover only one floor, two floors, or a dozen

floors. So you must pay for a roof, regardless. And you are left with only the expense of framing the second floor and building the walls. The roof must be built regardless.

So how do you build the second floor? For starters, you already have the joists in place. These are the ceiling joists for the first floor, which will work beautifully as floor joists for the second floor.

Starting with the assumption that the house is too high to move because of the electric and phone wires, you elect to have the roof removed. You can do this in two ways. One way, the easy way, is to simply cut part of the roof off; that is, you cut all the rafters four feet from the peak and discard the rafter ends and sheathing and roofing. Your house will look something like Figure 10-1. Don't be misled by Figure 10-1, because this is part of a house that had to be taken apart in order to move it. Most houses do not have to undergo this operation.

Or you can take the entire roof off and the house will look something like Figure 10-2.

You need to buy subflooring, which can be purchased in 4 x 8 foot sections or panels. Each of these will cost about $15 or less. You will need 40 of them, so your cost for subflooring will be $600, plus nails. Look at Figure 10-3. Although this is a porch floor, the exact same principles apply. Here I am nailing in the joists. Subflooring will be nailed on top of the joists.

Install subflooring by laying the panels across the top edges of joists and nailing the panels to the joists. Many people like to start by cutting the first panel in half and, starting at the corner, covering the first four feet. Then they use a full-length panel for the next eight feet. Continue the use of eight-foot sections until you reach the other end, where there will be a four-foot space. Use the other half of the panel you cut for this space.

For the next course, start with an eight-foot section and use eight-footers the entire distance. For the third course, cut a panel and install as you did for the first course. Repeat this process all the way across the entire house area.

Now start to frame the walls.

You start with the sole plate for the new floor. This sole plate is a series of 2 x 4 timbers nailed in place at the edge of the sills around the first floor ceiling. In other words, you buy 2 x 4s and lay them flat, end to end, around the entire area of the exterior of the house. Now you nail these 2 x 4s in place.

If you examine Figure 10-4, you will see double-spaced wall studs. Again, these studs are for the porch, not for the walls of an upstairs room. But the principle is still the same. Later we will add a stud between the existing studs.

Now look at Figure 10-5. Here we are starting to frame the actual upstairs area. In Figure 10-6 we have completely framed the upstairs area, but at this point we have not added the roof. In Figure

10-7 we have added the roof and re-installed part of the original siding.

**Figure 10-2**
*The house with the roof completely removed.*

**Figure 10-3**
*A sample of nailing in joists.*

This house looks rough, but we have simply closed it in to protect it from the weather. And remember that we bought the house for less than a dollar and had to collapse it in order to move it. Now we have added four rooms and 1,440 more square feet. If you figure the added space at $15 per square foot (and there is little hope you can ordinarily build for that figure today), we have increased the value of the house by more than $20,000.

**Figure 10-4**
*A sample of double-spaced studding.*

**Figure 10-5**
*Starting to re-frame the roof.*

Our next steps are to complete the siding work and add a chimney. In Figure 10-8 you can see how the finished work is starting to look. We still have to paint the house, but at this point we have less than $5,000 tied up in the cost of the house, cost of moving, and cost of restoring it, and that $5,000 figure includes the well and septic tank.

Now think about your house — the one you just bought and made arrangements to move. Suppose your house is 40 feet long and 32 feet wide. You buy 10 eight-foot 2 x 4s for the two long sides and eight 2 x 4s, also eight feet long, for the short side. When these are nailed in place the sole plating is completed, but don't nail them down just yet. If the 2 x 4s cost you $2 each, you have spent only $636 (including the $600 for subflooring panels), again plus nails.

Next you will need top plates. These will cost exactly the same as the sole plate and you will need exactly the same number of timbers. Your cost is now $672.

You will need more 2 x 4s for the top cap and the corner posts and braces, so if you buy 100 more timbers, you will pay $200, which brings your total to $872.

Now let's build a wall frame. Lay one of the 2 x 4s flat and mark off stud locations. At the end of the 2 x 4 mark off a space 1.5

inches long across the bottom side of the timber. Now move 16 inches from the end and mark the spot. Draw a line across the timber and then draw two more lines, each ¾″ on either side of the first line. These two outside marks indicate the location of the second stud.

Now do the same thing at the following locations: 32 inches, 48 inches, 64 inches, 80 inches, and 96 inches. This last location will be at the end of the timber.

The timber you just marked was the sole plate. Now mark the top plate. Lay it against the first one and mark it exactly the same way. When the marking is done, separate the timbers about eight feet and lay a 2 x 4 at each of the marked spots. Then nail down through the top of the top plate and up through the bottom of the sole plate and into the ends of the 2 x 4s in the middle.

When this is done, you have completed an eight-foot section of wall framing. If you prefer, buy longer 2 x 4s for the sole plate and top plate and mark off 12 or 16 foot timbers instead of eight footers, although there is no reason you can't stick with the eight-footers if you prefer.

At this point locate a timber, a board or another 2 x 4, for example, and plan to use it for a brace. Let helpers lift the wall frame section and position it at the very edge of the sill and nail down through the sole plate and fasten the sole plate to the sill.

Then use a level to see that the wall frame unit is a true vertical and nail the brace to the face of one of the timbers at each end. The other end of the brace should be nailed to a block which is nailed to the plywood subflooring.

When you build your next section, do it exactly the same way, and when you raise it, nail

**Figure 10-6**
*A roof completely re-framed.*

**Figure 10-7**
*The house with roof installed and walls closed in temporarily.*

the two end studs together for added strength. Build five of these units, and one side of the house is framed.

**Figure 10-8**
*The house with roof and siding completed.*

Now frame one end. Build four more of the units and raise them and nail them in place. At the corners construct a corner post in this fashion: Lay a stud 2 x 4 flat and cut three foot-long sections of 2 x 4. Nail one of these flush with the end at the top, another at the bottom, and the third in the center. Now nail another stud on top of these three pieces. Lay the unit on its side and nail another stud so that one edge is flush with the edge of one of the studs already assembled.

This corner post can be used in place of the single stud at the end of the wall frame. Such a construction will permit you to nail the two framing units together at the corners.

Complete the entire framing for the upstairs area. At the corners you can use metal bracing strips or plywood to strengthen the corners. The plywood is nailed to the outside of the framing and on both sides of the corner. Do this on all four corners.

Where you plan to have windows, do not use full-length studs. Instead, assuming that the window units will be 48 inches wide, omit two full-length studs and instead nail in a rough window frame at the height you desire it. Cut cripple (short) studs and nail these flush against the sides of the full or common studs. Then nail a length of 2 x 4 across the tops of the cripple studs.

At the top of the window there will be a header, which is a solid construction reaching from the top of the rough window opening to the top of the wall frame.

When the entire wall is framed and suitably supported with corner bracing, you can frame the interior walls. One workable plan is to determine what type of layout you want in the space and then use a measuring tape and a chalk line to lay out the rooms. If you do not like the results, you can wipe up the chalk and try again.

Assume you have 1,280 square feet, which is the size of the hypothetical house we started with. You could have four basic rooms with 320 square feet each. That is almost 18 feet by 18 feet, which is a nice sized room. But you don't have a hallway, a space for the stairs, or any closet space. If there is to be a bathroom upstairs, there has been no provision for it.

So you need to think out your options. One of these is a single huge room that would involve the entire upstairs area. This could be a monstrous game room, or family activity room.

However, most families could not make efficient use of such a room. So you could think in terms of two additional bedrooms and a connecting bath. Imagine the layout. On one end of the house there could be a corner bedroom, 16 x 12, and an eight-foot by six-foot bath connecting it to the second bedroom. In the other space left over between the two bedrooms there could be two large closets, one for each room.

In the remaining space you could have room for a stairwell, a hallway, landing, and a huge family room. Or there could be a study, office, or family library and another room used for a family room.

There are dozens of possibilities, and almost whatever you do would increase the value of your house greatly.

When you have decided on the layout, chalk the lines and then frame walls, just as you did before. Position the sole plate on top of the chalk line, raise the wall, and nail it in place. Do the same with the remaining walls. Frame the closets, baths, and other rooms as though they were full-size rooms. That is, keep installing studs either 16 inches on center or 24 inches on center, as many builders are now doing.

When all of the walls are framed, go back and nail top caps over the top plates. These top caps will tie all the framing units together and produce a strong bond capable of withstanding immense stress.

Once the plywood is used on the corners, you can use panels of insulation over the remainder of the outside walls, and you can install insulation between studs over all the outside walls.

When all framing is complete, you can frame the roof just as you would have done if you had simply put the roof rafters back up as they were when you started to work on the house.

You will need to add plumbing, wiring, and ceiling covering, plus ceiling insulation. There will be more work to do, such as wall coverings and floor coverings, moldings, painting, etc. There will be the cost of stairs as well, but you can build your own stairs for a fraction of the price the stairs would cost you if you bought them. Here we are talking about basic stairs, not an elaborate spiral staircase.

When we were setting our house up for occupancy, we priced a new set of stairs. The firm wanted more than $22,000 for the huge stairway alone, and suddenly the stairs that came

with the house began to look irresistibly good. We stuck with them and never once missed the stairs that cost far more than the sum total of our house, including the costs of moving.

Studies have shown that families which add a second story to their house increase the value of the house by more than $45,000. These families can, if they decide to sell, recoup about 97% of that cost. This means that you can live in the house for several years and still get nearly all the money back that you invested in improvements, even if the housing market does not rise in cost. With predictable appreciation you can not only get your money back but make a profit in addition.

Look at the figures. If you add $45,000 value to your house but you did not spend even half that money, you have made a rather handsome profit in case you decide to sell. When you figure the 97 percent regaining of the theoretical figure, you are talking about $43,650. But if you did most of the work yourself and you spent only $16,500, you have made a profit of $27,150, minimum, in the event you decide to sell.

With all building costs, you can figure that half the total cost is labor, so by doing the work yourself you save $22,500 at the outset. You can save even more by buying carefully where you can get the best deals and by cutting waste.

Incidentally, when you start to do any kind of repair or remodeling work that will involve a fairly large amount of money, go to the building supply store where you plan to buy most of your materials and ask for a contractor's price.

We did, and the store promptly gave us the discount when we told the manager that we were acting as general contractors for the house and would be in charge of all purchasing. We saved a large amount of money by this arrangement.

To give you a better idea of how much money you can save, we recently (within two weeks of this writing) decided to add a third bathroom to our house. Nationally the figure for simply *remodeling* a new bath runs more than $7,000, and we were able to add the entire bathroom for less than $900. So you can see that your own work can be done for about one-seventh or one-eighth the national cost.

Using this same figure, you could then add the upstairs to your house not for $45,000 but for $5,600 or so, which would make your profit or house value an even greater bargain.

In the following chapters there will be suggestions as to how you can handle the addition of:

a family room ($27,000 – $3,800);
attic bedroom ($18,500 – $2,640);
major kitchen remodeling ($18,000 – $2,585);
adding a home office ($7,000 – $1000);
replacing windows ($5,000 – $714);
replacing or adding siding ($4,500 – $642);
bathroom addition ($9,500 – $1,357);
deck addition ($5,500 – $785);
and minor kitchen remodeling ($7,000 – $1,000).

The first figure in each set of parentheses represents the national average for the projects. The second figure in the parentheses is the amount for which  you can do the work if you are willing to sweat and devote weekends to the jobs.

The next chapter deals with re-hanging the kitchen cabinets or buying and hanging new ones.

# Chapter Eleven
# Re-Hanging Kitchen Cabinets

In many houses available for moving, the cabinets in the kitchen (and elsewhere) may not be up to the standards you need. You have several options with regard to cabinets: you can take them down, strip off the old paint or stain, and re-hang them, or you can buy new ones and have them installed. If you take the latter suggestions, you will pay for the installation as well as for the cost of the cabinets.

A final pair of suggestions: Build your own cabinets, or buy new ones, have them delivered, and hang them yourself. You may have heard horror stories about how difficult it is to hang the cabinets, and you may even encounter cabinet makers who will not install cabinets on anything but new walls.

Do not worry about these scary tales. You can handle every step of the work and save yourself lots of money. Start with the idea of hanging new cabinets that you have bought and which the manufacturers delivered to your house.

First, before you buy, do some comparison shopping. Buying cabinets is in a sense like buying a new house or car. You can find a price range that will stagger you. You can easily spend $9,000 and up for cabinets, or you can buy them for $1,200 or less. You can build your own for about $300-$400, depending upon the materials you use.

In addition, you will pay an extra $400 or so to have the cabinets hung. The price may be much more than that if you have large cabinets and several of them.

If you want to hang your own, there are two easy ways to accomplish the work. First, you can mount the cabinets directly to the wall; second, you can mount plywood on the wall and then mount your cabinets to the plywood.

To mount cabinets directly, first locate wall studs. You do not want to attach cabinets which, loaded with canned goods and kitchen supplies, will weigh several hundreds of pounds, to the wall covering.

Be sure you are familiar with the basic terms. Wall studs are 2 x 4s installed vertically to provide the essential framing of the wall. Sometimes 2 x 6 timbers are used in extra-thick walls. These studs are nailed at the top to the top plate and at the bottom to the sole plate, discussed in a previous chapter. The studs are strong, and they will support huge amounts of weight. You are in great shape if your studs are spaced 16 inches on-center or closer. If studs are 24 inches on-center your wall is not quite as strong. Obviously 2 x 6 studs spaced 24 inches on-center will provide more strength than 2 x 4 studs spaced 16 inches on-center.

Wall covering, on the other hand, is any type of material used to cover the studs and to provide a wall surface. The most common types of wall coverings are gypsum board (or sheetrock), paneling, plywood, and boards. Often you will find that sheetrock is covered with wallpaper. Occasionally plywood is also wallpapered for a finished look. In rarer instances you will find that even carpet is used to cover walls, but where carpet is used some other form of wall cover is installed first.

Years ago, plaster was one of the most common wall covers, but the use of plaster has diminished in recent decades. You may, in fact, find that the house that you have just moved has walls that are composed of studding, lath (wood strips nailed across the studs horizontally), and plaster.

Here you may want to make a change before installing any of the cabinets. Plaster occasionally cracks when the house is moved, and attempts to patch the cracks are often unsuccessful. You may want to take it down and install new wall covering.

If you decide to change wall covering, you will need to take down the cabinets first. Do this by first unloading every item you can from the cabinets. A can of beans will weigh a pound or so, and by the time you include the bags of sugar, flour, and other kitchen supplies, you will find that you have a rather large amount of weight to handle.

When cabinets are unloaded, locate the screws or nails that hold the cabinets in place. If screws were used, start by taking out every other screw. If there are eight screws across the top, leave the corner screws and alternate screws in the series. Take out the lower screws until all that is holding the cabinets is the series of screws across the top.

Remove the interior or center screws and leave the cabinet hanging only by the end screws. Finally, determine which end of the cabi-

net can swing down more safely, and then remove the screw from the opposite end. As you do, use one hand to support the end of the cabinet. When the screw comes free, use both hands and slowly allow the cabinet to swing downward until the bottom end rests securely on the floor.

If the cabinets are not long enough to reach the floor, you can construct a makeshift bench by standing two cement blocks on end and laying a wide and strong board across the tops of the two blocks. When the bottom end is secure, remove the final screw and use one hand to keep the cabinet from toppling. Then you can lower it to the floor.

Using the method described above, one person can take down a large cabinet and not create undue risks to the welfare of the worker or the cabinet. If you have helpers, simply have two people hold the cabinet while a third one removes the screws. The two helpers can then lower the cabinet to the floor.

If nails are used to hold the cabinet (and do not use nails when you re-install the cabinets, because they do not hold well and they are extremely difficult to remove if you need to do so), you will need to pry the cabinet gently from the wall and then use a crowbar, wrecking bar, or hammer to pull out the nails.

Here's one way to handle the problem. Insert the blade of the crowbar under the edge of the cabinet. Choose a location that will show least when the cabinet is re-hung. Pick a spot under the cabinets or on the top, which is typically invisible from the floor area.

Insert the tip of the blade only an inch or so, and then pry gently. Move across the top and pry at three or four locations until the cabinet starts to separate from the wall.

Next, move to the sides or to the bottom and pry. This time, use a block of wood under the crowbar so that the weight from the pressure will be distributed and you will not damage the wall or the cabinet edge. Keep prying gently until the cabinet pulls loose from the wall.

It may be necessary to pry the cabinet out slightly and then tap it back into position. By doing so you will pull out the nails half an inch or so, and when you tap the cabinet back in place the nail heads will be exposed. You can then use a block of wood and a hammer or crowbar and remove the nails from the inside of the cabinet.

While the cabinets are on the floor you have the opportunity to strip the old paint or stain from the wood and to refinish the woodwork and replace any damaged doors, hinges, or handles. This work is much easier while the cabinets are in a handy, reachable location. You can take them to your workshop, if you wish.

When you are ready to re-install the cabinets, start by deciding which method you will use. If you wish to mount the cabinets directly to the walls, you must have a solid anchor for the screws you will use or the bracing mounts you will install under the cabinets.

Locate the wall studs and mark them so that you can see the marks when you are installing the cabinets. You can locate the studs by using a magnet to locate the nails used in securing the sheetrock to the studs, if the stud locations are not visible. Mark at least two nail locations and then use a chalk line to mark a straight line from the top of the wall to the bottom. The chalk will wash away easily after you are done, but it is vital that you know all stud locations behind the cabinet area.

Mark all of the studs as you did the first ones. Be sure that the chalk line strikes across the nail heads. If the chalk hits a nail, you are sure to hit the stud when you sink screws. I must stress the importance of stud locations. If you mount the cabinet with the screws sunk in paneling only, the weight of the cabinets will pull the screws loose and they will crash to the floor. Serious damage and injury could easily result.

When you are ready to mount the cabinets, measure the height of the cabinets, and then use the measurement to determine the exact location of the cabinets so that they will be at a perfect height for your needs. Have a carpenter's level handy for the steps in mounting the cabinets.

Start by erecting some type of scaffold that will hold the cabinets while you work. You can use 2 x 4s to build a quick and easy stand that is really a very high bench, if you have no one to help you lift the cabinets. Lift the cabinet, one end at a time, until the weight rests upon the stand you built. Now edge the cabinet back until the back of the unit touches the wall.

Measure again to be certain that the height is correct. If it is not, use blocks of 2 x 4s or similar wood to build up the height of the cabinet until you have it where it should be. When the cabinet is positioned where you want it, make a last minute check with the level to be sure that the cabinet is perfectly horizontal. Make any needed corrections.

When all is ready, drill small holes, slightly smaller than the shank of the screws, into the back of the cabinet at a spot over the studs. If you have trouble locating the studs, don't worry. After you have drilled the small hole you can look through the hole to find the chalk line. Then adjust the cabinet until the chalk line is aligned with the hole in the back of the cabinet.

You can also fasten one end of the chalk line to the wall so that the chalk line touches the first chalked line. Then pull the line across the top of the cabinet and down the front and back to the wall so that the line touches the chalk line below the cabinet. Align the screw with the chalk mark and drive the screw into the stud.

If you hit the stud with the first screw, use a level to be certain that you remain in a vertical alignment and mark the spot for the next screw. In this fashion you can sink the screws in all the vital locations and the cabinet is essentially hung.

Use screws that are long enough and strong enough to hold the cabinet once it is mounted. Ask your hardware dealer for his suggestions. If you are left on your own, I suggest a screw that is at least 2.5 inches long and has a thick shank.

You can buy screws with a Phillips head or slot head. My personal preference is the Phillips head, because you have a better seating of the screwdriver point and the screw head. You are less likely to ream out the screw head and render the screw useless.

If you choose to use plywood (and I think that this is by far the easiest way to handle the job) for mounting the cabinets, stand the cabinets in the center of the floor and then stand a panel of plywood behind the cabinet. Pencil a line around the two sides and the top of the cabinet. Be sure the line conforms to the exact shape of the cabinet. Use half-inch plywood or thicker.

When the mark is made, saw along the line. The result should be a section of plywood that is the same size as the back of the cabinet.

Now mount the section of plywood. You may want to stain the edges the same color as that of the cabinets before you hang the plywood so that there will not be a clash of colors when the work is completed.

Locate studs as before. You can stand the plywood on the floor and hold it against the wall where you will mount the unit of cabinets. Strike a chalk line or make a pencil line vertically along the stud locations.

Drill pilot holes two inches from the top, two inches from the bottom, and in the center of the plywood along the chalked line. Do the same along every stud line.

Mark a pencil or chalk line to designate the top, bottom, and sides of the plywood. Start the screws for the two top corners and run them completely through the plywood so that the points stick out the back side by a quarter of an inch or so. In the middle section run two small nails (8d or 10d) and have them ready to drive. Hold the plywood section in place. Check to see that the edges match pencil or chalk marks. Once you are certain that the line-up is correct, drive the nails into a stud. Do not sink the nails completely; drive them in just far enough that they will hold the plywood section.

Check again to see that the match-up is still good. If it is, start sinking screws. When all others screws have been sunk, remove the two

small nails and replace them with screws. Before you leave this stage of the work, use a level to see that the plywood is vertical. It is possible that the wall is not perfectly true, and if you need to do so, push small shims under the plywood to bring it out to the point that you get a level reading.

Now you are ready to raise the cabinet to its proper place. To do this, use the scaffold or bench described above and lift the cabinet to the shelf that will hold it. If you are working alone you can use two wide boards (six inches or so) located so that one is at the one-third point of the cabinet width and the other is at the two-thirds point. Place one end of each board on the scaffold and the other end at the back of the cabinet. Set the cabinet onto the bottom ends of the boards and begin to work the cabinet up the boards. You can lay the cabinet down on the boards until you reach the top, if you wish.

With the pre-drilled holes in the back of the cabinet lined up with the marks indicating stud locations, drive two nails part-way into the plywood, deep enough to hold the cabinet while you check for perfect alignment and then drive in the screws until the cabinet is securely mounted.

Before you complete installing the screws, you might wish to use the level and also a square to be sure that you have not lost the true level reading. Check the corners of door frames to see that the frames are still true. If there is a problem, loosen the screws slightly and correct the problem. You will need to use new holes for the screws before you re-tighten them.

Cabinet units for the floor need no special installation. All you need to do is push the cabinets into position, check for level and squareness, and leave them. The weight of the cabinet will hold the unit in place.

When your house is in place, before you make the final plumbing connections you might decide to add a bath or half bath to the existing floor plan. Chapter 12 details how to use a small amount of space to convert a closet to a half-bath.

# Chapter Twelve
# Converting a Closet
# to a Half-Bath

It has long been said that no house can have too many bathrooms. It seems that no matter how many there are in the house, there are times when the number is at least one too few.

If you buy and move an older house, chances are good that the house will have too few baths. Part of the reason is that a few decades ago, many people farmed or worked away from home, and bathing was not deemed as important as it is today, when one shower a day often seems inadequate. Too, in older days, parties were not as frequently given as they are today.

So if your older house has only one or one and a half baths, and if there are three or more people who will live in the house, you may wish to look at several bathroom options. First, common sense and economy dictate that bathrooms should be placed back-to-back when possible, in order to keep from running pipes long distances.

Economy of plumbing is one reason for the bath placement, but there is the added problem of hot water. If hot water must be pumped from the hot water tank to the other end of the house, at times a distance of 50 feet or more, you have the double problem of waiting for the water to heat and the waste of hot water.

For example, when you turn on the hot water tap in the bathroom, the water is pumped to the faucet, and you must wait while the 50-foot distance is covered by the hot water that must force the cold water from the pipe. Then, after you turn off the tap, the hot water in the pipe then is wasted, because it cools and must in turn be pumped out before more hot water can be pumped. So you have a waste of time, water, and energy to heat the water.

Logic, then, dictates that you use back-to-back bathroom arrangements or, as a reasonable alternative, to install one bath directly above the other. In this way you at least shorten the distance the hot water and waste must travel.

Before you buy the house and make arrangements to move it, look into the bathroom situation. Check to see how much trouble it will be to add another bath. The house we moved had been built in pre-Civil War days, and therefore no bathrooms had ever been a part of the house. So we had to decide how to install bathrooms without disrupting the entire traffic pattern for the entire house.

One solution we reached was the bath-on-top-of-a-bath approach. Above our ground-floor bathroom there was a closet that wasn't badly needed. And before anyone yells that just as a house can never have enough bathrooms, it can also never have enough closet space, let me remind you that according to the building code in many areas any room that has a closet can be considered a potential bedroom. And the number of bedrooms governs the size of the septic tank required to meet the code.

So don't worry about losing a closet, unless you have an absolutely critical shortage. Instead, think of it as gaining a new bathroom. For closet space you can always use one of the old-fashioned clothes cabinets that are free standing.

In our particular case the closet in question was located directly above the downstairs bathroom, so our plan was to take down the wall containing the door to the closet and move it out about three feet, enough to permit room for the bath.

Here's a good tip when you are taking down and rebuilding walls: look at the direction of the tongue if the wall covering is tongue-and-groove lumber. If the tongue points downward, then start work at the ceiling. If the tongue points upward, start with the floor molding.

Assume you are starting at the top of the wall. In our case, and in the case of many closets, the interior wall is not really finished. Instead, in so many cases there are panels of thin plywood covering the studs. Work from inside the closet and take down any wall covering on the inside.

Then use a magic marker or similar implement and start at the top and number the boards in the outer wall. Starting at the left, arbitrarily, number the boards in the top course 1A, 1B, etc. Then the next course is 2A and 2B, etc. Continue all the way to the floor. When you take down the boards, lay them in a secure place and, if possible, in the order in which they were taken down.

To take down the boards, use a small crowbar, hammer, or even a large screwdriver, and pry the ceiling molding loose and set it safely aside. Then, starting at the top of the board, on the groove side, slip the blade of the pry bar under the board and gently pry outward. Be careful not to crack or splinter any boards, unless they are worthless.

Work your way down the wall until you have only the studs and electrical boxes remaining on the wall. Before you take down the studs, remove the electrical boxes and secure them.

Some people are terrified of burglars; others fear spiders or poisonous snakes or mad dogs. My personal terror is electricity. So before I touch an electrical outlet of any sort I take about every precaution known to man.

Experienced electricians insist that if you turn off the wall switch, the light fixture is not "hot." If you turn off the breaker for the outlet circuit, the circuit is dead and will not be harmful if you touch the wires.

Here is the Williams approach: I turn off the wall switch or the circuit breaker, and then I plug in a lamp or radio or even the electric mixer. I refuse to take chances that the lamp bulb is burned out, or the radio is broken. I assume that if all three items which played or worked well in the next room now will not work, the power to the outlet must indeed be off.

Then I get my wife to do the work.

Only when I am confident that the outlet will not and can not shock me, I remove the box by prying the nails holding the box until there is an inch of play, at which time I use a pry bar to remove the entire box.

If you wish, you can attach the box temporarily to a stud in another wall, or in some place where you are not likely to brush against it. You will need to turn the circuit breaker back on, so that you can have light while you work. Figure 12-1 shows a mount being installed on a stud in a bare wall. Note the use of the board held in the right hand. This board is the thickness of the wall covering that will be used later (described in detail in the next chapter). Note that the board extends past the outer edge of the mount slightly. This is so there will be room to install the light fixture so the mount is enclosed to prevent any possible shorting out of the circuit.

In Figure 12-2 you can see the mount as it is being nailed to the stud. There are two nails holding the mount, and these run through small openings that are so designed that you can drive the nails without smashing the mount.

In Figure 12-3 you see the wire as it is fed through the hole or knock-out in the back of the mount. Be sure to leave adequate wire so that when you connect the light fixture you will not run short. It is much easier to cut off any surplus than it is to try to stretch the wire.

If you need to remove the wall outlet and the wire has been run through a stud, while the power is still off loosen the screws that hold the actual sockets and remove the screws. Now take out the socket and make a careful note of how it is wired. You will notice that black wires attach to black, red to red, etc. Note how the ground wires are connected.

If you need to do so, make a rough drawing of the exact locations of the connections. Now take the loose wires, and pull the wires through the hole in the stud. Reassemble the outlet and attach the box safely in its new location. If it is to be installed again in the same wall, nail the box to a safe spot as far from your work center as possible.

Now take down the studding. As before, pry the studs gently to see if you can force the nails to give a little. You can also tap the back side of the stud with a hammer and drive it back in the direction opposite that of the nails. Tapping the stud end an inch is usually sufficient. Now tap the other side, but do not hit the nail heads. Drive the stud end back to its original position.

What happens here, you can hope, is that the nails will be pulled from their original position, and then when the stud is tapped back in place the nail heads will be left sticking out. At this point you can use a crowbar or hammer to pull out the nails.

Before you start to work, number the studs as you did the wall boards. Set each stud you remove safely aside and leave it there until it is needed again.

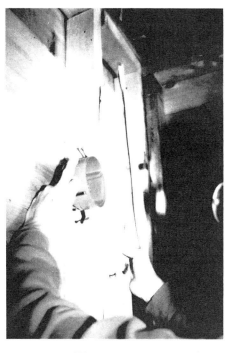

**Figure 12-1**
*Using a wall board to determine position of mount.*

**Figure 12-2**
*Nailing mount to bare stud.*

When all the studs are removed, pry up the sole plate, which is the 2 x 4 running along the floor and on which the ends of the studs rested. Then pry down the top plate, which is the 2 x 4 that runs along the top of the wall. The top plate is where the other end of the studs had been nailed. At this point the wall has been completely dismantled. Now you need to move it.

**Figure 12-3**
*Installed mount with lead-in wire.*

To do so, measure out from one corner of the closet to the point in the adjacent room where you wish to reassemble the wall. Mark the spot with a pencil and note the exact distance. Then go to the other corner of the closet and measure out exactly the same distance and then mark the spot.

Strike a chalk line from one mark to the next. If you are working alone, tap a nail into the subflooring just deeply enough to hold the chalk line end. Loop the chalk line over the nail and

pull the line to the other mark. Hold the chalk line so that it is stretched firmly, lift the line with your thumb and forefinger, and then let the line go so that it snaps against the floor.

The line you have just chalked represents the outside wall of your new bathroom. Locate the sole plate and, if you have not already done so, tap the pointed ends of the nails until the nails have been driven through to the other side of the plate. Lay the sole plate so that the outside edge is aligned exactly with the chalk line.

Drive the nails back into the sole plate and into the subflooring under it. Now measure from one corner of the closet to a point that is the exact distance you measured earlier for the location of the sole plate. This time, however, measure from the top of the room to a point on the ceiling in the adjacent room. Mark the spot and then measure out from the other corner, just as you did before.

Now chalk a line between the two points. Think of the whole operation as laying out a sole plate on the ceiling. The only real difference is that you are now positioning the top plate rather than the sole plate.

Install the top plate exactly as you did the sole plate. At first you should drive two or three nails partly in, and then use a plumb bob or level to be sure that the top of the wall is in line with the bottom. If you don't have a plumb bob, you can stand a stud so that the outside edge of the stud aligns with the outside edges of the sole plate and top plate. Then hold a level against the side of the stud.

If you get a good reading from the level, move to another spot and check again. If the reading is again good, your top plate and sole plate are vertically true and you can finish nailing up the top plate.

Now re-install the studs. Nail in the studs in the same position they were in when you dismantled the wall. Use different nail holes for greater holding power. Space the studs 16 inches on center. If you have trouble nailing the studs in place, cut a length of wood just long enough to fit between the stud and the wall adjacent to it. Lay the short length of wood in place and drive nails into the opposite side of the stud. The piece of wood will prevent the stud from moving backward as you nail. If you need to do so, nail the short piece to the sole plate in order to keep it from moving as you nail.

Because the studs have already been used, some building codes forbid their use a second time in a load-bearing wall, but if you are building only a partition wall you will probably run into no problems. In order to add strength to the wall frame, however, you might want to nail the studs from both sides. You will need to use the toe-nail or angle nail approach, which you can accomplish by holding the point of the nail against the side of the stud and angling the head upward to about a ten o'clock or two o'clock position. Then drive the nail in at an angle so that the point of the nail penetrates the sole plate or top plate by about two inches or slightly less.

If you have trouble starting the nail at an angle (the nails tend to slide down the stud surface rather than penetrate it) you can hold the nail at a right angle to the stud and drive it straight in a quarter of an inch or so. Then use your fingers to bend the nail upward or downward, depending upon where you are nailing, and drive the nail as you normally would.

When the studding work is completed, you will need to install the outlet or switch box as quickly as possible. You do not want to work around a dangling live electric box. Again, turn off the power to the box or switch. Don't take chances. Drag out the lamp or radio or blender or whatever will tell you that the box is dead.

Unwire the box as you did before, again using drawings or notes to keep the wiring details certain. Now, run the wire through the stud and again wire the box as it was when you first removed it, as shown in Figure 12-4. You are now ready to re-install the box by holding the box in its original position and then driving the nails into the stud.

**Figure 12-4**
*Threading new wire through studs and to old fixture.*

At this point you can put up the wall covering that you took down and saved for use at this time. Install the wall boards in the reverse order of the way you took them down. You can probably use the same nails and the same nail holes that were used when the wood was installed originally.

When the wall covering is back in place, you need to frame the doorway to the bath. You already have a rough door opening that was once part of the closet wall. Now add the header. This is, in walls like this, usually only two 2 x 4s nailed together to strengthen the door opening.

Now install the doorway framing units. Install these just as they were when you took down the wall.

At this point you have a bedroom complete with all of its walls and wall coverings, and you have a doorway that leads into the new bathroom. Inside the bathroom you have four walls that have no wall covering. Here you have a choice of using the fast and inexpensive sheetrock or gypsum board. One panel covers 32 square feet. In other words, the single panel of sheetrock will cover the expanse of four feet, or three studs. Actually, the edges of the panel will cover half of the outside studs and all of the inside studs.

While sheetrock is easy and fast to install, the work is somewhat dusty and the sheetrock tends to break and crumble if you mistreat it. Do not try to saw it. Instead, use a razor knife and cut along a straight edge held in position. The blade of a square works well, as does a length of board. Cut through the paper bonding and then you can break the sheetrock where you wish.

When you nail up sheetrock, do not nail close to the edge. If you do you will crush the edge and destroy the integrity of that portion of the panel. After the sheetrock is installed (and there is more detail elsewhere in this book) you need to apply the tape and compound, then sand the compound. These latter stages require considerable care and time, and you need to wear a mask to keep from inhaling the dust particles created by sanding.

You can also cover the walls with tile, paneling, or boards. In our house we chose to use boards of knotty pine on all four walls and on the ceiling. But we cut and dress our own lumber, and we can do the work at virtually no cost.

If you use boards on the walls, you need, because of the moisture in a bathroom, to use a sealer such as one of the newer polyurethane products that protect against dampness.

At this point, in fact, even before you install the boards or other wall covering, you need to take care of the basic or rough plumbing. Chapter 13 offers suggestions on how to plumb a new bathroom. It also adds to some ideas

presented here. This chapter is essentially about the methods of handling the work involved; Chapter 13 is more specific in terms of the actual implementation of the work.

# Chapter Thirteen Basic Plumbing for a New Bathroom

Throughout this book I have stressed that the house you buy may be a fantastic bargain in its own right, but if you want to undertake a few basic improvements, the house becomes far more valuable. Our house contained two bathrooms when it became our property, and we had no real need for a third bath.

However, the upper level of the house contained two bedrooms that were isolated from the remainder of the house. This meant that overnight guests had to descend the stairs in order to have access to a bathroom, and such a trek is not always welcome. In fact, it is sometimes downright troublesome.

Our problem was that there was no real space suitable for a third bath. Even if we settled on a half-bath, we'd have to reduce the size of the bedroom drastically, and we did not want to take such a step or make such a sacrifice.

Finally, as described in the previous chapter, we decided that an existing closet was the answer. As the house stood, you entered the bedroom and on your immediate right there was a recess in the wall, and at the end of the recess there was a closet. So we decided that we could tear out one wall of the closet and move it so that it was flush with the doorway into the room. In this fashion we could have a small half-bath, if

we could work out the problems presented by the knee wall, or the slope of the roof and the way it created an outer wall four feet high and slanting upward to normal height.

**Figure 13-1**
*Taking down the old wall.*

What we did you can do. All you need to do is modify the half-bath we built to suit your own house and your own family's needs. The first step, if you are converting a closet or similar small space to a half-bath, is to take down the wall and door framing for the closet. Figure 13-1 shows the final stages in the removal of the wall. As you work, remove the wall covering with care so that you can put it back up when the job is completed inside the closet area.

Remember to save and re-use the wall covering by numbering each piece as you take it down. You can lay out the wall assembly exactly as it was installed in the wall, and then you can put it back up in the same manner. Figure 13-2 shows the short wall laid out upon a bed. The wall is upside-down, and the sections nearest the lamp will be the first to be nailed back into the wall.

When the job of taking down the wall is completed, you have an open space that, if the bathroom is carefully planned, you can convert into the needed half-bath space. Figure 13-3 shows the room area with the wall completely removed.

**Figure 13-2**
*Laying out the wall boards
so they can be replaced later.*

**Figure 13-3**
*The former closet, now ready to convert into a half bath.*

The next step is to stretch a chalk line from the existing wall to the wall on the opposite side. Be sure to measure the distance from the back corner of the closet to the corner of the existing wall, and then measure the same distance from the other back corner of the closet to the point where the wall should be constructed. Figure 13-4 shows the chalking of the line.

Rebuild the wall frame so you will be certain of where your boundaries are. Be sure to measure the width of a toilet tank to be sure you have room for it before you start to cut holes in the floor. Because there has never been plumbing of any sort in the upstairs rooms, it is necessary to cut out a section of the subflooring in order to gain access to the lines that will be connected to the new bath. In Figure 13-5 you can see the distance needed for the toilet and tank. You can also see the wall frame that has been rebuilt.

**Figure 13-4**
*Chalking the line for the bathroom wall.*

Once the distance has been settled, cut out subflooring to provide a means of installing the pipes to carry away the waste from the toilet. Figure 13-6 shows approximately half the space needed for the hook-ups.

Hold the end of a pipe against a joist and mark around the pipe to provide the exact size for the hole to be cut through the joist. You should keep the weakening of the joist to a minimum, and, as you can see in Figure 13-7, the pipe is not large enough to cause problems, yet it is sufficient to carry away waste.

When the circle is drawn, one easy way to cut a hole in the joist (space is so limited that you cannot get a saw into it) is to drill a series of holes around the circle and then use a hammer, as shown in Figure 13-8, to knock out the wood.

Run the pipe through the hole, as shown in Figure 13-9, and then add the fittings that will

allow the pipe to curve, in a sense, so that it will meet the existing line. Figure 13-10 shows the fittings ready to install. Note that one opening, the one on the right, is for the commode, and the other is for the sink. In the center the two lines drain into the existing drain line.

Figure 13-11 shows the connections as seen from above. The open line on the left is the toilet connection and the other leads to the sink. To the right of the photo you can see the waste line extending upward into the room for later connection with the lavatory.

When this much work is done, you cannot do any more until you have covered the walls, at least up to the point that is slightly higher than the bathroom lavatory cabinet and toilet tank will be. If you install the facilities now, you will not be able to work behind them to nail up the wall covering.

Remember that the drain lines for the downstairs plumbing are in the basement, and the new lines will have to run down through a room. Measure carefully in order to get the hole and pipe and supply lines as close to the wall as possible, as shown in Figure 13-12.

Now go into the basement or under the house and locate a spot directly under the lines. Saw through the line, as shown in Figure 13-13, and then install the joints for the lines from the upstairs bath. In Figure 13-14 you can see the process of joining the pipe once the access joints have been installed. In Figure 13-15 you can see the pipe coming from upstairs and also the heating or "sweating" the supply lines for hot and cold water after the lines from upstairs have been joined to the existing lines. The term "sweating" means that in order to join two copper pipes or tubes you first sand the pipes, inside and out, depending on how they are to be fitted, and then coat the surfaces of the pipe ends with a paste that reacts to heat by becoming a sealant, and then you heat the pipes with a torch and hold a length of solder so that as the heat melts the solder it runs around the pipe and as it cools it fuses the two metals.

The next steps that must be taken before the toilet and sink can be installed are those of flooring the room and then building in the walls, at least high enough to rise above the toilet tank and the cabinet. You must install the flooring because until you do you cannot seat the toilet.

**Figure 13-5**
*Drilling a hole before cutting out subflooring.*

A good idea is to lay out flooring in a loose pattern to see how your supply of flooring will last. In order to keep waste at a minimum, determine how many pieces of varying lengths you will need to make one full course without having to cut any pieces. Notice how in Figure

13-16 the lengths are laid out so that no cutting at all will be necessary.

**Figure 13-6**
*Cutting out subflooring in order to install pipes.*

If you find that some of the pieces have bowed and will not fit together, you can force them gently into place by rigging up a device such as the one shown in Figure 13-17. Here we nailed a small length of 2 x 4 to the subflooring and then propped a short length of board between the block and the flooring. Next we used a pry bar to force the flooring into position. While one person holds the flooring in place, another nails it.

Notice in the same photo the boards used in the wall. Only days earlier these "boards" were part of a pine tree that had been partially uprooted and was leaning against another tree. The tree could not live in such a condition, and we cut it, then used a chain saw to cut the trunk of the tree into boards.

We then used a planer to smooth one side of the boards to a perfect finish. We then bolted the boards together, with small strips of wood between boards to let air circulate, and we stored the boards in the basement near our wood stove. In a remarkably short time the boards were dried out, and the bolting process kept them from warping as they dried. We added a couple of coats of polyurethane and when the sealant dried we installed the boards.

**Figure 13-7**
*Drawing off the circle for the waste lines.*

Be honest. Have you ever seen any boards in your life that were more beautifully finished than these? The boards we cut are behind the flooring. The other wall is made up of boards bought from the lumber supply house. The commercial boards cost dearly, while the boards we cut cost us less than two dollars to build three walls and one ceiling for the half-bath.

The flooring, too, is recycled. We pulled the lumber from an old house, ran it through a planer, and sealed it. It is oak, and it would have cost an enormous amount if we had bought it. The floor of the small room cost us less than fifty cents.

In Figure 13-18 you can see the entire oak floor and part of the wall we built from "home-made" boards. The process of cutting our own lumber with a chain saw has intrigued me and pleased me so much that one of my near-future books will be devoted totally to chain-sawing and making useful items for the house, none of which will cost more than a few pennies.

Also in Figure 13-18 you can see the supply lines for the hot and cold water. Note that the stubbed-off lines extend upward through the floor by about a foot. You must keep the stubbed pipes fairly long to permit the installation of a cut-off and also connections to the sink.

In Figure 13-19 you see the installed cabinet for the bathroom sink. Note that the handles on the door are on the wrong side. This is the way the cabinets are shipped for three reasons. First, the handles are not as likely to be lost or picked up by someone in need of handles as they would be if the handles were loose. Second, there is less chance that the handles will be damaged by bumping into obstacles or that the handles themselves will be damaged by other obstacles. Third, the handles inside the doors permit smaller shipping cartons and easier stacking.

Before the bathroom walls are erected all the way to the top of the room, you need to take care of any wiring you plan to do for the room. In our case we had a receptacle on the outside wall of the closet, which meant that there were no wires inside the bathroom area. We needed one light switch, one receptacle, and one light fixture for the small room.

So we first determined the spot for the light-fixture box and nailed it to a stud. Then we took down the receptacle on the outside wall and after we moved the wall, we drilled holes through studs. After buying 25 feet of 12-2 wiring, we threaded the wire through the studs and into the knee wall. We then connected the wiring to the wiring inside the receptacle (all this with the power OFF, please understand) and, in short, we moved the receptacle to the inside wall of the bathroom. We ran wire to a wall switch just inside the door, which we also made ourselves, and then to the light fixture above the cabinet and sink.

**Figure 13-8**
*Knocking out the circle after
drilling holes around it.*

Elsewhere in this book there are some statistics relative to the cost of home improvements, and you will note that the cost of adding a bathroom is nearly $10,000. A man I met recently told me that he was able to add a bath in his house at a cost of only $3,000.

If you can do the basic electrical, plumbing, and carpentry work yourself, you can add your own bath for far less than $1,000. In fact, you can do it for less than $300, and increase the value of your home by thousands of dollars. I am speaking of a half-bath at this point. If you add a full bath, it will cost you about $700-800 for the shower unit, toilet, sink and cabinet, pipe, waste lines, and carpentry and electrical materials. Still, if you can get a $10,000 value for less than $1,000, and in the process you increase the value of your home by no less than $7,000, you have spent your time, energy, and money well, and you will benefit greatly if you sell the house.

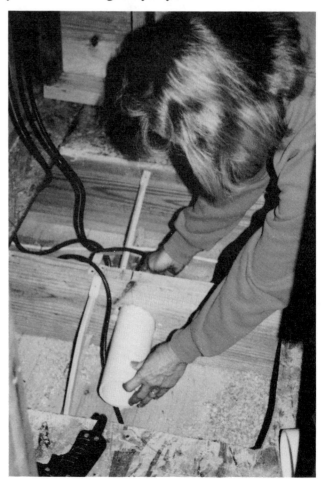

**Figure 13-9**
*Installing the waste lines through the joist.*

**Figure 13-10**
*Waste lines with connections for sink and toilet.*

**Figure 13-11**
*Waste lines for sink and toilet installed.*

**Figure13-12**
*Waste line coming through downstairs
room near wall.*

**Figure 13-13**
*Cutting through waste lines in basement.*

**Figure 13-15**
*Waste line from new bath connected and supply line "sweated."*

Here are a few final pointers concerning the carpentry phases of your half-bath or full bath. Your toilet tank will stand about 25 to 28 inches high, and you will need to cover the walls behind it. If you use boards, as we did, you can use the poor end, if there is one, on a board behind the toilet tank or the cabinet, and the flaw in the work will never be seen. If you must join boards, there is always the chance that you will not get a perfect match, so measure out your lumber so that you can do the joining work behind the toilet or cabinet.

The same is true of flooring. If you have a piece of floor material that is blemished, work it out so that it will be under the cabinet.

You can also use poor cuts at the doorway, because later you will cover the ends with door facing. Always try to hide defects in your work, rather than discard a length of flooring or board that is excellent except for the one tiny flaw. Cut waste and you will cut expenses.

**Figure 13-14**
*Banding waste lines to re-connect them.*

**Figure 13-16**
*Laying out flooring for best use of materials.*

**Figure 13-17**
*Using pry bar and fulcrum to position flooring.*

**Figure 13-18**
*Finished floor, walls, and supply lines for sink.*

**Figure 13-19**
*Cabinet positioned, ready for sink and connections.*

# Chapter Fourteen
# Paneling Walls

When you have your house moved and resting on foundation walls, you will need to think in terms of covering walls. Few elements of construction work of any sort can be more depressing than the constant sight of walls in need of repair.

It was stated earlier in this book that houses do not tend to suffer from the moving activities, but often the house was in poor repair before you ever saw it. You can be wonderfully lucky and find a house that is in excellent repair, and when that house is moved there is virtually nothing to be done in repair work.

But just as often the houses in the best physical shape are the ones most bidders will put their money on, and you can find yourself in a bidding war. Worse, you can either bid too high and pay far too much for the house, or bid too low and someone else buys the house for a dollar or two more than you offered.

It's a gamble, at best. But you must ask yourself which is the more feasible route for you to take: Paying $10,000 or more for a house that will cost another $10,000 to move, or buying a house in need of repair for $250 and paying $5,000 to have it moved and another $2500 to make the needed repairs?

Remember that the older houses are often constructed of the best timbers, while newer houses are often made of poor materials. In recent months I ordered a small load of timbers, among them 2 x 4s, 2 x 6s, and 2 x 10s. When the lumber arrived, I insisted on sorting through it and I refused to accept nearly half of the shipment. Some of the studs were so poor that I'd have hesitated to use them in a house for a dog I didn't even like.

But what if you are a building contractor who will not live in the house he is building and who isn't paying for the lumber? You, as the contractor, know that the client will never see the studs that are filled with defects, so you don't delay the work process by insisting on high quality in the lumber. Five years later that house is already showing signs of deterioration, and the walls are beginning to sag or the floors are dropping, if only slightly. These warning signs are hinting strongly at what the house will be like in another five years.

On the other hand, some — certainly not all — of the older houses are made from select timbers. Joists and rafters are of heart pine, not sapwood. In the house we moved I needed to cut out a small notch in a monstrous joist, and I used a handsaw for what seemed like hours and never damaged the wood noticeably.

So you are back at the decision-making stage. This chapter is included in this book because I think I know what answer many readers will select: Buy the older house in need of minor repairs and save 50 per cent of the cost of the total job.

Even if the house you buy is in good repair, you may not like the decorations and perhaps will elect to change them. Whatever your reasons may be, if you wish to install paneling, this chapter will provide details on how to proceed.

Your first consideration is what type of wall coverings you want on your walls. You can find dozens of possible coverings at the building-supply store. Your primary considerations will be cost, thickness, and design. You can get 4 x 8 panels of birch, oak, pecan, and an amazing array of others, all in imitation or veneer styles.

Prices will range from special sales at $8 or so up to $25 per panel. You will also need to buy colored nails to match the paneling, but this cost is negligible.

To figure how many panels are needed, you must measure the height of the room. Assume that it is eight feet high. One panel will reach from floor to ceiling without cutting or fitting. Now measure the length of each wall. If the wall is 12 feet long, then three panels will cover the entire wall.

Go a step beyond. Two walls are 12 feet long and two are eight feet. You will need six panels for the two long walls and four panels for the short walls. For less than $150 you can panel the entire room, if you can find paneling you like at reasonable prices. If the room is 18 feet by 18 feet, you will need 18 panels. You will use four panels on each wall, plus two feet from a fifth panel. The two-foot section left over from the wall will fill in the remaining space on the next wall.

If your paneling costs you $20 per panel, your cost for the room will be $360, plus a little extra for nails and taxes. Sheetrock is, on the surface, at least, less expensive. Remember, though, that after you put up the sheetrock you must add the compound and the tape, plus extra hours of work at sanding and finishing and painting.

One of the tricks in any type of building is to minimize waste, and you can keep waste at a minimum by marking and cutting exactly and by using smaller or scrap pieces to fill in over the doors and windows.

To install the paneling, you must start by cleaning up the existing walls. This means taking down the plaster, if that is the wall covering that was used, and disposing of it. If the walls are covered with sheetrock, you may leave the sheetrock in place and install the paneling over it. The only problems you have to worry about are the possibility that the paneling will make the walls too thick for the molding or baseboards, if you have any, and the possibility that the walls are uneven.

Assume that you have an uneven wall created by studding that was installed green or sappy and has now bowed outward until the wall is irregular. Paneling can cover the problem, but it can never conceal it. The correction methods are either to replace the studs or to correct them.

The easy way is to knock out the defective studs and nail in new ones. But if you want to correct the bows, cut lengths of plywood 3.5 inches wide. This is the width of a stud. Use plywood that is one-half inch thick or five-eighths. Start pairs of nails every two feet along the length of the strip.

Now push the bowed stud back into the wall area until the bend is corrected. While holding the stud in its correct position nail the plywood to the stud.

If the stud refuses to bend back into shape, nail a length of 2 x 4 to the floor (not if you have hardwood floors!) six feet from the wall. The strip should run parallel to the wall.

Now position a 2 x 4 or other timber so that one end rests against the length of wood and the other end rests against the stud, near the top.

Now push the timber firmly down against the stud, and then use a hammer to drive the timber downward until it forces the stud back into alignment.

While the stud is in its corrected position, nail the strip of plywood to the stud. When the brace is removed, the stud will stay in place. The key is that plywood is made up of several layers of thin wood that cross each other. Because of the cross-cross effect, you cannot bend the plywood in either direction because half the wood layers resist the movement.

If you are uncertain about the trueness of the wall, hold a straight 2 x 4 across the studding about halfway between floor and ceiling. Check to see if the timber touches every stud. If it does not, there is at least one stud that sticks out too far or bends the opposite way. If there is a discrepancy of only an eighth of an inch, you will be all right.

When you are certain that the walls are correct, you can start to nail up paneling. Usually you nail paneling directly to the studs rather than to lath, so start in a corner. Hold the panel up in its correct position and fit it as snugly as you can into the corner.

This is very important! Hold a level against the outside edge of the panel once it is in position. Check the corner to see that you have a perfect fit. Any mistake that you make at this point will continue as a mistake across the entire wall. You must absolutely correct the first panel if you want any of the others to be perfect.

If you have a helper, get him to hold the panel in place while you step back to check the fit. If you have no helper, use a prop of some sort to hold the panel in place. Examine the fit both at the top and at the bottom.

If there is a space of two inches or so at the top of the panel and the bottom corner fits well, you can correct the problem in the following manner. First, measure to be certain that you have the exact distance. Remember: The space is at the top, so you must make the correction by starting at the bottom.

Lay the panel flat on a work surface that will permit sawing. Use a pencil to mark the top end of the panel, but mark it on the back. Assume that it is the top right corner that is giving the trouble. On the back of the top right corner mark the panel.

Then move to the bottom and measure over two inches (or whatever the exact distance was at the top). Then strike a chalk line from the two-inch mark at the bottom to the upper right corner of the panel.

Remember that you should turn the panel over before you cut it. Circular saws cut upward, as a rule. This means that the wood of the panel will splinter slightly on the top side. So you want the top side facing upward. This is why you mark the upper right corner — so you will not become confused when you start to mark the cut. The chalk mark should be on the back if you are using a circular saw.

Keep in mind that the upper right corner as the panel stood in place is now the upper left corner when you turn the panel face-down. Start your mark at the bottom and end it at the point of the upper corner. Then saw along the line. When you position the panel in the corner, it should fit perfectly.

Now for a reversal of thought. If you are sawing on a table saw, the blade turns in the opposite direction, as a rule, from that of the circular saw. So you will need to cut the panel with the top side facing upward. That is, the side that will be exposed to the room should face upward.

From this point on it is essentially a matter of nailing the panel in place. One note of caution: beware the perfect fit from top to bottom. Any time you are cutting a length of wood or panel to fit into a designated spot, do not try for a totally exact cut. Here's why: If you cut the piece slightly too long, you will then need to cut off one-eighth of an inch. This is difficult for most people to do, and you wind up marring the end of the piece of material so that it looks unacceptably bad.

If your ceiling is exactly eight feet, the panel should fit precisely, although you may have to maneuver it a few ways before you get it in place. If the panel is slightly too long, it will bow out in the center, and no amount of nailing will correct the problem. There will always be a noticeable defect.

Cut off a quarter of an inch, rather than an eighth. When you stand the panel in position, use paneling nails and nail, as stated before, to the studding. Start at the outside edge and drive a nail at the top, center, and bottom. Remember that the edge of the panel should cover only half of the edge of the stud. The next panel must be nailed there, too.

Step back and look at the fit again. If the fit is good, go ahead and nail to all three studs, driving a nail every eight inches or so up and down all studs. If the fit needs further work, take the panel down. The easiest way is to pry it outward and pull the heads of the nails through the panel itself. If you try to pull out the nails you will likely scar the face of the panel, and three tiny holes will not show at all. In fact, you can later drive other nails into the holes.

The next panel should fit precisely against the first one. Nail it up in the same way.

When you come to windows and doors, the best bet is to take down the window and door trim and fit the paneling under it. If you try to cut the paneling so that it fits snugly against the trim, you will likely make a cut that is not perfect and which will show.

If possible, when you come to doors, cut the piece so that there is a cut-out for the doorway. That is, do not cut straight through the panel from top to bottom. If you do, the point where the two cut pieces join will be noticeable.

With the door trim down, measure from the edge of the last panel installed to the edge of the door frame. Then mark the panel for a cut of the same distance. Measure from the ceiling to the top of the door frame and mark the panel. You will then cut out an upside-down and backward L that will fit snugly into the remaining space.

Then re-install the door trim, and not even an expert can spot the cuts.

Do the same at the windows. Take down the trim, measure, mark, and cut, and then nail in the paneling. If you must cut a panel lengthwise, try to make the cut along a seam. Otherwise the cut marks will be clearly visible.

If you must cut outside the seam area, try to fit the piece of paneling so that the cut edge will butt into a corner or be hidden under window or door trim.

When all the paneling is installed, you may notice obvious misfits at ceiling and floor areas or in corners where cut edges are visible. You can put this worry from your mind, because you will install corner molding to conceal the corner cuts, and you will install ceiling molding and floor molding or even baseboards of the old-fashioned type on the floors.

A special word of caution. When you are driving paneling nails, take care not to drive the nails in too deeply. When the hammer peen strikes the laminated surface of the paneling, there will be a clear scar left. Nothing effectively covers the marks, so your best bet it not to make them in the first place.

Neither do you want to leave nail heads sticking out of the paneling, so you must develop a light touch that will drive the nail heads flat with the surface of the panel but not damage the panel surface.

There are three essential ways to handle the problem of scarring the paneling. The first of these is to develop a light touch with the hammer, particularly in the final strokes. Tap lighter and lighter as the nail head nears the paneling surface and let the final strokes be little more than pats.

A second method is to use a much smaller hammer. You can buy very light hammers for this use and similar purposes. The major difficulty with the lighter hammers is that if you are accustomed to using a heavier tool, you will tend to be inaccurate with the lighter version until you become accustomed to it.

A third method is to use a punch. This is a small slender tool that can be struck from either end. Place the small flat end of the punch squarely atop the nail head and use the punch to sink the nail to its final depth. Hold the punch steadily in one hand and tap the end with the hammer. Take care not to drive the nail head in too far. If you do, the head will penetrate through the entire panel and the nail will not hold.

If you decide to add rooms, as suggested in an earlier chapter, in order to increase the value of your new old home, you will need to install flooring. Chapter Fifteen offers suggestions on some basic ways to floor a room.

# Chapter Fifteen
# Re-Flooring Rooms

In an earlier chapter it was mentioned that you may wish or need to collapse part of the roof peak or later decide to add rooms upstairs. You would collapse the roof only if you needed to avoid low bridges or an unusual number of electrical or phone wires.

But you might decide to add an upstairs room or two if you wish to increase the value of your new home even more than you had previously imagined. In your work you might find it necessary to re-floor (or floor for the first time) some rooms in the house. In this chapter you will learn how to remove old flooring and then use it later in a new room or again in the same room.

You can take up old flooring, which is what we did with the part of our house that we could not move, and clean it up and then re-use the flooring later to produce beautiful floors. You may recall from earlier discussion that our house had servants' quarters connected with the back of the building. It was impossible for us to move the extra quarters, and we had to salvage as much of the add-on building as we could.

Here's what we did and what you can do. Take up the molding and baseboards first. You can do this by slipping the blade of a screwdriver or small pry bar under the molding and prying it

up. Nearly all molding is held in place by finish nails, which are only thin wires with tiny heads.

As you start to pry up the molding, move slowly. Do not try to rip up huge lengths of molding by brute force. Instead, pry up a section only five or six inches long. Then while holding the section pried up, use another small pry bar or screwdriver and move over another six inches. Pry up again, and then move the first pry bar over six inches past the first one. Keep up this pattern across the entire length of the room.

As soon as you take up a length of molding, which is often referred to as quarter-round molding, remove the nails and store the molding in a safe place. When the molding for an entire room has been taken up, remove the baseboards, if there are any. Use the same methodology for removing the baseboards.

In older houses these baseboards were often nearly a foot wide, and the old wood is extremely valuable, if it was kept in good condition. Exert great care so you will not crack or break the baseboards.

One of the best methods I know for removing baseboards is to use the long and heavy screwdriver again, or the small pry bars. You will need to start in a free corner. By this I mean that when you stand in the corner and look down at the baseboard, you will see that one of the boards butts into the other. You cannot remove the back board first. Instead, work on the one that butts into the other one.

Starting five or six inches from the corner, work the blade of the pry bar under or behind the baseboard. Start with an inch or so of penetration, and then place a short length of board or 2 x 6 under the shank of the pry bar so you will not damage the wall covering.

Pry out slightly, only enough to work the blade under the baseboard slightly more. When you are able to pry out the baseboard two or three inches, slip a short length of 2 x 4 or similar type of wood behind the baseboard to hold it out from the wall.

Then start the same pattern you used for the molding. Pry out a section and then move the 2 x 4 or 2 x 6 down as far as you can. Then pry another section and repeat the process.

When all the baseboards are removed, you can start to take up the flooring. Determine if you possibly can which direction the tongue of the flooring faces. The nails will be in the tongue, so this is the side of the lumber you need to work on first.

Start, obviously, at the wall. Often the final board will not be an exact fit and there will be a crack between floor and wall. Most builders do not worry about the crack because baseboard and molding will cover it. Insert the blade of the pry bar into the crack  and gently pry outward and upward. You may have to damage one end of the first board in order to get it up.

Once the first flooring board has been taken up, the remaining boards will come up easily. Insert the pry bar under each board and pry upward and outward. The nails were probably driven into the boards at an angle, and they must be pulled out at an angle to keep damage at a minimum.

As you did before, pry up a short section of board and then use a second pry bar to pry at another point. You may find that the boards will not snap back into place, so the second pry bar may be unnecessary.

Once you are a foot or so from the wall, you can use the crooked end of a crowbar and pop the boards out instantly. Push the blade under the board and then push down on the handle of the crowbar, and typically the boards will come free without your having to exert any real effort.

When you have the boards taken up, remove the nails and store the boards until further use. You may have two-foot up to four-foot sections of oak flooring. This flooring is, like the other hardwood flooring, valuable, so take good care of it. If you have the short lengths of flooring, you probably have a high grade of lumber. The short lengths are cut in order to avoid the knots and other defects in the wood, so you probably have some fine flooring. Do not treat it carelessly.

At this point it is time to discuss a small investment that may prove to be of great value to you in your work. I am referring to a small and portable planer. You can buy a very fine portable planer for about $280, and while this is not a trivial amount of money, you get a great deal of value for your dollars.

Once your flooring is up and all the nails have been taken out (and I mean *all* of the nails and nail heads and carpet tacks and staples — anything metallic) you can set the planer on the proper thickness and run the wood through the planer.

If you have never used a planer, most of the common portable machines have a cylinder inside that can be lowered and raised by use of a wheel or crank. This cylinder has two blades installed in it, and when you lower the blade to the proper point and run the wood through, the blades will shave off one-sixteenth, one-eighth, or even one-fourth inch from the top side of the wood. Do not attempt to take off more than one-eighth of an inch of wood at any pass through the planer.

If there is a nail hidden in the wood, the metal will damage the blades severely or ruin them totally. For this reason, do not take your wood to a professional planer. The operator of the machine will probably warn you that if there is any damage to the blades, you will be expected to replace them. And no matter how careful you are, you will possibly miss one nail.

If you damage your own blades, you can handle the problem in one of three ways. If the damage is minimal, you can run a whetstone over the edge of the blades and remove irregularities. If the problem is too great, you can use a broad file and run it over the blade until the problem has been removed.

The final solution is to buy new blades, which for a portable planer will cost no more than $15 or slightly more for a set of two blades. The blades can be sharpened in the same manner as described above. Clamp the blade in a vise and hone or file the cutting edge until it is again sharp and even.

When you use a planer, a workable method for planing the old oak flooring is to clamp the planer to a work table with enough room at the front to stack unplaned wood and enough room at the back to stack the finished wood.

Before we began work in earnest, we decided to build a quick table for use in planing. We used some old scrap wood (See Figure 15-1) that had I had earlier cut for rough window framing in an out-building. The wood had never been painted, and we could see that there were no nails in it.

We planed down some of the thick boards to a more useful size and then shaped them for our needs. With these boards we built the frame for our planer table. See Figure 15-2. When the table frame was completed, we planed and shaped more boards for the work surface, as shown in Figure 15-3.

When the table was done, we shaped a wide and thick length of lumber and nailed it to the table top. Then we mounted the planer to the wide lumber, as shown in Figure 15-4. When that was completed, we added wheels for easy maneuverability.

When you are ready to use the planer, raise or lower the blades by turning the wheel or crank. Insert one end of the flooring barely into the open space and lower the blades until the metal frame contacts the wood. Turn on the machine and the rollers and blades will pull the wood through the work area and the flooring will emerge on the back side of the machine.

You will not believe the difference one pass through the planer can make in a length of wood. A rough, dull, and actually ugly length of flooring enters the planer, and a shiny, smooth, and beautiful section of wood emerges. The planer in effect does three jobs: It shaves, smooths, and sands the flooring. The wood is ready to use when it is planed. For a great lesson

**Figure 15-1**
*Discarded lumber to be used for making a table.*

in the use of this piece of equipment, lay an old section of flooring beside a newly planed section and see the difference. In Figure 15-5 you see an old length of lumber beside a second piece of lumber that looked exactly like the first only seconds earlier. After the planing was done, the two pieces of wood bore little resemblance to each other.

In Figure 15-6 you see several lengths of oak flooring, all of which looked deplorable before we planed them. The wood is now ready for the sealant and then for installation.

When you have planed all of the flooring, you are ready now to re-install it. You simply reverse the method of removing it, in a sense.

Start at one wall and push the first section of flooring into the corner and against the wall. Hold it firmly in place while you drive cut nails into the angle formed by the tongue. A cut nail is one that has four flat sides; it is not round like other nails. The purpose of cut nails is to keep splitting and splintering at a minimum.

Here is a slight but valuable tip for carpentry work with wood you cannot afford to damage. If you are using finish nails in very thin wood, you can usually keep from splitting the wood if you will stand the nail with the head on a metal or otherwise hard surface and with a hammer hit the point of the nail rather gently but firmly. You in effect dull the nail; you flatten the point.

As hard as it is to believe, the dulled or flattened point will drive through thin wood without splitting it. Note that the cut nails have flat points, or, actually, no points. Many bars are used in log houses to drive through the logs to hold them together, and the totally flat ends will

**Figure 15-2**
*Completing the framing of the table*

**Figure 15-3**
*Adding the table top.*

punch through the wood rather than split it. That is the entire principle behind the cut nails.

Your major difficulty may be the fact that your flooring, which is as strong and beautiful as ever, may have cured so hard that you will split it in spite of every precaution you can use. The answer to the problem here is to drill a small pilot hole before you nail. The hole, which should be slightly smaller than the thickest part of the nail, will let the shank of the nail pass through it without splitting, and there will be enough bind to keep the nail tightly driven inside the wood.

So, with the first piece of flooring, its end pushed into the corner and the tongue side pushed firmly against the wall, ready for nailing, drill the holes, if necessary, and drive the nails at the proper angle.

Remember that when you are nailing at an angle, hold the nail so that the widest flat side is in the angle formed by the tongue, and the shank of the nail is held at an angle equal to ten or two o'clock, depending on which side you are nailing. When the nails are driven almost flush, stop hammering. Do not crush the tongue or the top surface of the wood.

If you crush the top surface, you will have an unsightly mess which hours of sanding will not correct. If you crush the tongue, the next piece of flooring will not fit. The groove will not slip over the tongue, and a snug fit cannot be accomplished.

Instead, stop at a safe point and use a punch for the rest of the operation. The punch is so manufactured that you can hold either point against the nail head and drive the punch, or you can lay the punch flat against the nail and hit the shank of the punch with the hammer. The thickness of the punch is exactly the size of the groove formed by the tongue. Use the punch and save yourself worry and work.

Some older flooring, as well as new, is end-matched as well. Check to see if yours is. The ends fit together in a manner that is similar to

**Figure 15-4**
*The planer mounted to the table.*

**Figure 15-5**
*Old (right) and "new" lumber, one that has just been planed (left).*

that of tongue-and-groove wood. See Figure 15-7 for a view of end-matched flooring. Fit the ends and the tongue-and-groove at the same time. Then nail.

**Figure 15-6**
*An assortment of oak flooring lengths just planed.*

Sort out your flooring by lengths. By doing so you can reach into the right stack and pull out the length you need. Make a quick inventory of how many pieces of what lengths you have. Then calculate which combinations of pieces you will need to make one full course of flooring.

If your room is 12 feet wide, you can use three four-foot lengths, two six-foot lengths, four three-foot lengths, or other combinations. Do not use all of your longer units of flooring at first and then have to use a patchwork of two-foot pieces for the remainder of the floor. If you have an ample supply of various lengths of flooring, use two six-foot sections for one course and in the next use three four-foot sections.

Why not four three-foot lengths? Because your second length will end at the same place your six-foot length ended. You do not want this kind of pattern. Never let two pieces end at the same point. You need the bonding effect created by the overlapping of the units of flooring. This is similar to the overlapping and bonding of bricks or cement blocks in masonry work.

Do not nail extremely close to the ends of the flooring. Use one nail every two feet in longer lengths. If you are using two-foot sections to fill out a course, use at least two nails. Never use a unit held in place by only one nail. Keep nails four inches or so from the ends of flooring.

Alternate lengths across the entire floor. When you reach the opposite end of the floor, you may have a space too large for one length of flooring to fill. Do not worry if you have an inch or so of space left over. The molding or the baseboard (some people in fact use both: baseboard plus quarter-round molding) will cover the small space between the final flooring and the wall. If you have a space too small for the flooring to fit into it, your answer to the problem is to measure the space (and it may not be the same at both ends of the room: the room may not be perfectly square, or you may not have nailed the flooring as snugly on one side as the other, or the flooring may not have been precisely the same width) and then mark the flooring and chalk a line along the entire length of the flooring. Turn it over so that the top is facing down, before you mark the piece. Keep in mind that when you flip the flooring you must modify your chalking, as you did with paneling.

Use a circular saw and rip the flooring. Be sure to leave the groove side on the flooring. You may need to slant the final units of flooring in order to get the best possible fit. Tilt the flooring just enough that the groove can make contact with the tongue and gently press the flooring flat.

You may need to lay a short piece of 2 x 4 on the flooring and then tap the 2 x 4 to force it into the space. If the fit is entirely too tight, remove the flooring and rip off another half inch.

You cannot angle-nail the final flooring. You can deal with the problem in two easy ways. The first of these is to drill a tiny hole near the wall and use a finish nail to hold down the flooring, and the second is not to nail at all but to let the molding or baseboard hold the final flooring in place.

The next chapter discusses how to take down and re-install ceilings.

**Figure 15-7**
*End-matched flooring.*

# Chapter Sixteen
# Completing Ceiling Work

This chapter may not be important to many people who move houses, if the move is a one-story house that has needed no real modification. But if you need to take down a wing or other part of the house, you should plan to salvage anything of value in the section of the house you are taking down.

Salvaged lumber is valuable from at least two important viewpoints. First, you can often sell the materials, even if you have no use for them yourself. Across the country many people leap at the chance to tear down old buildings, and then they store the timbers and dimension lumber until they have a use for it or until they can sell it.

In fact, I know one man who had the chance to demolish part of an old mill building that was to be moved from the area. The man hauled off load after load of timbers, some of them four inches thick and 12 inches wide and over 20 feet long. He built an entire house out of the discarded materials.

Assume that the ceiling is good in a room that must be taken down before the house can be transported. When I say "good" I mean that the ceiling has value as lumber, not that it is simply in good condition. A ceiling covered with one of the commercial fiber tiles is worthless, if it must

be taken down. The tiles will break and crumble and they cannot be used later. The same is true of plaster and sheetrock, for the most part.

Plaster cannot be taken down at all, except in pieces, and the only thing you can do with it is to haul it to the landfill. The sheetrock will be so damaged that there is little other than some patching work that can be done with it.

The ceilings I speak of are those made up of the old-fashioned beaded lumber or tongue and groove lumber or good, solid boards. You can take these ceilings down and salvage the lumber and use it later.

If your ceilings are the beaded style, you must be very careful when you remove the thin strips of wood, some of which are only half an inch thick or even thinner. Start the removal by taking down the molding, as you did in the previous chapter. Take the molding down slowly and carefully and remove the nails in each piece as soon as you haul it down. If you do not, you will soon have a rickety stack of wood that will break if anyone steps on it and which will be so tangled that you will damage the boards as you try to extricate them for later use.

Keep a nail bucket handy. Do not simply pull nails and let the nails fall to the floor where they will be ground into the flooring as people step on them. The nails could wind up in someone's foot.

When the molding is down, look for the section of ceiling that has the largest crack between ceiling and wall. This is very likely the place where the final piece of ceiling was installed. And in all salvage operations of this sort, you work backward. The last piece put up is the first piece taken down, and the final piece you take down will be the first one installed.

If the ceiling boards are old, they will have cured to a very brittle degree. You can expect some damage, but you can keep it at a minimum by exercising a few basic precautions.

Do not use a large crowbar or pry bar. Instead, use one that is no more than a foot long. Try first to work the hooked end into the crack, and then try to work the end of the hook under the board. If you can, push it under as far as you can, and then pull down with very light but steady pressure.

If the board does not give, increase the pressure. Be sure that the fulcrum of the hook is resting on a joist or rafter so that you will have a solid foundation. If you still cannot get the board to give at all, place a thick short section of a board behind the curve of the hook and increase pressure.

If your luck holds, the nails will either pull through the board and free the board, or the nails will pull out of the joist or rafter. The worst case scenario is that the board will break and split. If this happens, move to another part of the board and try again.

Usually you can get the end of the board loose. When you do, you will have about 16 inches of free board. At this point locate a length of 2 x 4 about as long as your forearm, and when you pull down the end of the board shove the 2 x 4 under it so that the 2 x 4 is resting against the adjacent ceiling. Push the 2 x 4 (or 1 x 4 board, if one is handy) as close to the next joist as you can get it.

Now with one hand push up gently but firmly on the end of the ceiling board, and with the other hand work the hook of the crowbar under the board at the next joist. Continue to push up gently with one hand and pull down with the other.

The anticipated result will be that the pressure on the loose end of the board will cause tension and pressure on the next nails, and, coupled with the downward pressure of the crowbar, you should be able to pop the nails loose.

Continue doing this all the way across the room. When you come to the end of a board, do not yield to the temptation to pull down and rip the nails loose. By doing so you can damage the end of the board so that you will have to cut off several inches before you can use the board.

When the first course of boards is taken down, you should have an easier time with the following boards. You should still work slowly and with great patience, but the progress will be much improved and the damage less.

If you find no easier success, try this technique. Use a longer crowbar this time and stand a short block of wood on top of the next board and against the joist. Now position the crowbar so that you have the hook in your hand and the claws are pointing down. The angle of the crowbar end rests upon the short block and the point of the crowbar is against the subflooring of the attic.

Jerk the crowbar downward so that the angled end bumps against the block of wood, which in turn bumps against the board. This method works well, once you have enough room in which to use the longer crowbar.

If you don't have a crowbar handy, use a length of 2 x 4 as your pry bar. A four- or five-foot length works well.

If the ceiling is made up of tongue-and-groove lumber, you will work in essentially the same way. Again, look for the widest crack and see if there is a tongue on the board. Or, if not a tongue, a smooth surface where the tongue had been cut away. If you see a groove, you know that you are on the wrong side of the room. Move to the other side and begin to work.

If the fit of the board you need to remove is too good, so that you cannot work the blade of a pry bar into the crack, you can try this method, which will damage the end of the board to a slight degree but can save the rest of the board.

The final board had to be installed with nails near the wall, near enough that the molding covered them. (The edge may not even be nailed at all; perhaps the molding supported the edge of the board, in which case you can take down the board with little effort.)

If there are nails, locate them and then hold a claw hammer so that the claws would straddle the nail head if the head were a little exposed. Tilt the claws so that they will dig slightly into the wood and then use a second hammer to hit the head of the first. The force of the blows will cause the claws of the first hammer to dig into the wood until the claws grasp the head of the nail. You can then pull the nail in the traditional manner.

When the house is ready for you to put back the ceiling, nail it up in reverse of the order you took it down. Always start as you started the flooring, and remember never to allow two boards to end side by side on the same joist. You start with the groove to the wall so that the tongue is in position for you to nail to it.

There are some tricks and techniques that can be used to install tongue-and-groove lumber on either ceiling or floors. These were not mentioned in the flooring chapter because there is no point in discussing the same material in two different chapters, and whatever you find in the ceiling chapter that will help you, the same principles will apply to flooring.

Because ceiling work is often harder than flooring work, this material was placed here. It relates to the difficulty in fitting tongues and grooves together.

You will find that grooves have been crushed in the work process, and there is no way the tongue will fit into the badly damaged groove. Here is one method that may help. Start at one end of the board where the groove is good, and

select a foot-long section of tongue and groove wood and fit it together so that the tongue fits into the groove neatly.

Holding the section of board tightly against the longer board, use a hammer to drive the shorter board along the entire length of the longer board. The tongue of the shorter board will clean out the groove of the longer board and will force the groove back to its normal open position.

If the bottom of the groove is damaged and the top remains in good condition, you can use a pocketknife or plane and cut off the bottom groove. Then when you position the next board in place, the tongue will fit under the top part of the groove, which will hold the tongue in place.

If nothing else works, you can always use your pocketknife and cut away any part of the tongue that is crushed and simply will not fit no matter how you try to make it. If you must, and if you cannot do without the board, you can actually cut off all of the tongue. You will give up the advantage of tongue-and-groove lumber, but you can use the piece at the wall where the absence of the tongue will not be noticed.

One of the worst problems you will face is that of warped boards. Sometimes, when boards have been stacked for a long time, they will bend and will not straighten. So you are left with the options of discarding them for firewood or finding a way to use them.

Here is the way. Imagine that you have a straight and true board installed, groove facing out, and the next board is warped so that when one end of the tongue is in place the other end of the board sticks out six inches from the other board.

This is an extreme case, but you can see that if the solution will work here, it will work in virtually every other case.

Fit the ends together and nail the end of the warped board in place, using the cut nails and diagonal or toe-nailing to hold the board, just as you did with flooring. Now locate a block of 2 x 4 and nail it to the bottom of the joist near the end of the board. The 2 x 4 block should be within two inches of the warped board end.

Now find a long 2 x 4 and position the end of it in the space between the warped board and the short block. Wedge the end of the long 2 x 4 tightly and then, holding the board high above your head and extending away from the end of the warped board, walk sideways so that the angle pressure of the long 2 x 4 will force the end of the warped board back into place. You can exert tremendous force with the long 2 x 4, and the tongue and groove board will give until the fit is perfect. Continue to hold the long 2 x 4 in place until your helpers nail the board securely in place.

What if you are working alone? You can tie the end of a short rope over the end of the long 2 x 4 and then pass the rope over a joist and pull it back to you. Now stand in nailing position and, after starting your nails, pull the rope so that it in turn pulls the end of the 2 x 4. You can tighten up as much as you need to, and then you can hold the rope with one hand to keep the board in place while you drive the nails.

If there is only a slight warp of one to two inches, which is far more realistic, you can set up the same arrangement as described above and then you can use a crowbar instead of the long 2 x 4. Start your nails and have them ready to sink, and then you can push with the crowbar until the board is aligned perfectly and then hold the board in place while you nail. See Figure 13-17 in Chapter 13 for a photo of this process.

What if you want to put up sheetrock or ceiling tiles? The tiles are easy. You will need nailers, which are long strips of boards installed at right angles to the bottoms of the joists. You should start with a nailer flush against the wall and then install the others at 12-inch intervals across the entire room.

If you need to do so, you can use a circular saw to rip 1 x 4 boards into two-inch strips. You can also use half-inch boards, because the tiles weigh very little and will not pull down the nailers.

Measure the room. If it is exactly 12 feet or any number of feet, with no inches left over, you can start by cutting the first tile exactly in half. Start in one corner and install the half so that it fits snugly into the corner. Make sure that both edges are snug against the walls.

If the room measures at a strange distance, for example 14 feet and eight inches, you will have a total of 176 inches. You will need to divide the eight-inch distance into two sections of four inches each. So nail up a four-inch section of a tile and then install the other tiles until you reach the end of the course, where you should have a four-inch space remaining.

In other words, divide the extra distance in half and cut tile sections to fit the space. Use the smaller sections at each end of the course of tiles.

Depending upon the tile, you may have to use sheetrock nails tight against the wall for the first tile. The molding will cover the nail heads later.

Then install a full-size tile. You will see that the edge is manufactured so that the tiles are edge-matched. Insert the lip of the second tile into position and then staple the other end to the nailer. Continue across the entire room until you reach the other wall, where there will be a six-inch space. The other half of the tile you cut will fit here.

On the next course you can start with a full-length tile and install it. You will now note that the tile will fit into the side of the first tiles. You will continue to staple as before.

On the third course, again halve a tile and proceed as you did on the first course. Continue this pattern throughout the entire room. By doing so each tile will bond to half of two other tiles, and you will have a neater and stronger ceiling.

If you are putting up sheetrock, you will need a helper or two, or you will need to construct a special helper out of some scrap lumber. If you have assistants, proceed in the following way.

Check all joists to see that all of them are either 16 inches on center or 24 inches on center.

If the joists are not spaced correctly, the ends of the sheetrock panels will not end on top of a joist and you cannot nail them in place. If you must do so, add joist surfaces by "scabbing" a timber to existing joists.

Scabbing, as the term grossly suggests, means adding a surface to an existing area. If your joist is only an inch or so off center, simply nail a 2 x 4 or larger timber to the side of the joist. If the distance is greater, for example three and a half inches, nail up blocks of 2 x 4 or larger lumber and then nail a long 2 x 4 or larger timber to the blocks. Be sure to use five or six blocks so that you will have ample support for the new timber.

If the joists are spaced correctly, as they should be, start in one corner and, after cutting a panel of sheetrock in half, nail up the first half. Take care that the edges of the panel are snugly fitted into the corner.

Follow the half-panel by a full panel. Continue with full panels all the way across the room. In a bedroom two panels may be more than enough to cover the space. In our house with its very large rooms (some of them about 40 feet long), we needed five full panels to span the distance.

While someone holds the sheetrock in place, drive special sheetrock nails through the sheetrock, about an inch from the edge if space permits, and into the joist. When the nail is fully driven, hit the nail head a last time to dimple the sheetrock surface. This dimple is to allow later for compounding to cover the nail heads.

Nail everywhere you can within reason. That is, drive a nail every foot or so along all edges where there is a joist to drive into, and then drive nails in the center of the sheetrock panel along joists.

For the next course, start with a full panel and continue to the end of the room. Continue in this manner until you reach the other side of the room.

At the other side, if you do not have a four-foot space, you will need to cut a panel. If you have a two-foot space, cut a panel in half, lengthwise, and make two units from a panel. If the space is three feet, you will have a waste of one foot.

You can always measure the room both ways to see how the sheetrock can best be used. If the room is 14 feet long by 12 feet wide, then install panels along the 12-foot section for a waste-free use of materials, and then use the two-foot sections to complete the work. You should nail up sheetrock, when you can do so without undue difficulty, across joists, not parallel with them.

Chapter 17 includes suggestions on how you can install sheetrock unassisted. The job is not easy, but it can be done.

# Chapter Seventeen
# Installing Sheetrock Unassisted

Why a full chapter on installing gypsum board or sheetrock alone? Try the operation for a few minutes and you will see why any help you can get is welcome. A panel of sheetrock is not only heavy but awkward as well, and the position in which you must work doubles the discomfort and problem.

First, the panel is eight feet long and four feet wide. You must lift it over your head and work it into exact position. And then you must hold it in place while you nail it.

On the surface the task seems impossible, and it very nearly is, unless you use some work-saving suggestions that will make it possible for you to free both hands while the sheetrock remains in place.

Again, though, why a chapter on working alone? The answer is simple. Often you will not have a helper. If you and your mate are installing sheetrock and if one of you is ill or otherwise unavailable, the work must stop until both of you can return. While you wait, valuable time is elapsing.

So this chapter is devoted to the topic of helping you to do the work alone. You start by analyzing the situation. How high is the ceiling? Measure to get an exact figure.

If the ceiling is exactly eight feet high, you can deduct half an inch to three-quarters of an inch for the thickness of the sheetrock panels. Your initial task now is to construct a sheetrock holder from some lumber that is available. You will also need a hammer, a saw, some nails, and a C-clamp. The latter tool is one of the most valuable assets you can possess while you are working alone. It may not be worth its weight in gold, but it's close. The C-clamp in effect gives you an extra hand.

Your lumber can consist of 2 x 4s, 1 x 4s, 1 x 5s, or any similar-dimension lumber. Start by laying out two 2 x 4 lengths of two feet each. Set these lengths side by side and four feet apart. Now lay two more lengths of lumber (1 x 4s will work well for this stage, or 2 x 4 lengths work equally well) across the first two pieces and at the ends. You have formed a basic square with the four pieces.

Nail the top pieces to the bottom ones, so that if you lift one piece of lumber the entire assembly will rise with it. Now, assuming that the assembly stands 2.75 inches high, locate two 2 x 4 lengths that have a combined length of about 110 inches. To the top of one 2 x 4 length nail a four-foot length of 1 x 4 board so that the 2 x 4 is in the center and the board reaches out on either side. Remember to nail the board to the top edge of the 2 x 4, not to the side of it at the top.

At the basic square, stand the second 2 x 4 so that you can nail the end of the 2 x 4 to the cross piece at the back of the square. When you are finished, stand the assembly so that the 2 x 4 points upward. Straighten it so that it is a true vertical, and then run a brace piece from the front unit to the 2 x 4.

To review, you now have two simple assemblies. The first is a 2 x 4 or similar lumber with a board nailed flat to the top of it. The second assembly is a basic square with a 2 x 4 extending upward and a brace supporting and steadying the 2 x 4.

Here's how you use the device. Stand the basic square where you plan to work, and then hold the T-shaped assembly so that the two 2 x 4s overlap each other. Open the C-clamp wide enough to reach over the two 2 x 4s and tighten the clamp just enough to hold the 2 x 4s together.

Check the height of the T-frame of the upper part of the device. If it is too low, loosen the clamp and raise the T-frame until it is within three inches of the bottom of the joists where you will nail the sheetrock.

To use the device, stand it with the T-frame in position and the clamp tightened securely this time. Raise a panel of sheetrock enough that you can slide the end of the panel between the top of the T-frame board and the joists. You can let the end rest on the T-frame board while you go to the other end of the sheetrock and push and lift as you slide the sheetrock over the T-frame until the panel rests above the middle of the frame.

You can check again to see how much too low the sheetrock panel is. If you need to do so, you can loosen the clamp just enough so that you can slide the top 2 x 4 upward until you have a snug fit of the sheetrock panel against the bottom of the joists.

Now turn the sheetrock panel loose and it will be held in place. If you need to make a minor

adjustment in order to get the panel in the perfect position, you can do so. You can also start to nail the sheetrock into place.

When you read the above suggestions, your first impulse is perhaps to think that this is a great deal of trouble. Actually, nothing could be farther from the truth. The assembly can be made in only a few minutes.

If you have the lumber ready, it will take ten seconds to place the first pieces in a parallel position. In another ten seconds you will have the second pieces in place. In a minute you will have the four pieces nailed together, and in another two minutes you can have the 2 x 4 upright in place. Within about five minutes the basic square can be completed, and within another two or three minutes you can have the T-frame completed.

All told, you will invest 15 minutes in making the device, and when you load the first panel of sheetrock onto it, the entire process will take no more than a minute or two. So the time factor is negligible.

What is important is that you are able to get yourself set up to work within 15 minutes, and you can salvage an eight- or ten-hour day by doing so. Once you get the hang of using the device, you can put up sheetrock nearly as fast as two people working in tandem can.

When you are finished with the first panel, loosen the C-clamp and lower the frame an inch or two and then slide it down into position for the second panel, and then you will repeat the process. If you wish, you can make a second version of the device and you can position the sheetrock easier and faster. Your work will be smoother and more effective. But if you do not wish to take the time, you can get along reasonably well with the single device.

You can cover an entire ceiling of a small room within a matter of an hour or two. If you are putting sheetrock on a wall, you can handle the job alone without any special help. All you need to do is measure first to see that the eight-foot panel will fit satisfactorily between floor and ceiling and then you lift the panel and set it in place. You can push it into the corner and, using a level you placed handily before you lifted the panel of gypsum board, check the edge of the panel for a true vertical reading.

Correct any problems as you did with paneling. If, when you have a level reading, there is a gap of two inches at the top. take the panel down and lay it on a work surface. Measure over from the bottom — not the top — two inches and then strike a chalk line from the two-inch mark to the top corner. Then cut off the two-inch section that tapers down to the point.

If the gap is at the bottom, then mark the spot at the top and strike the chalk line from the top to the bottom point. This simple measure will result in good fits in the corner under nearly all circumstances, the exceptions being when the wall is actually wavy or bowed out at the center, and this, thankfully, is a rarity.

Remember that the corner panel must always be vertically true or you will have every following panel untrue. When the sheetrock is nailed up along the straight and uninterrupted walls, you will need to install portions of panels around windows, doors, recesses, and alcoves.

These are not problem areas. You simply measure the space and cut sheetrock to fit. Where there are alcoves or recesses, fit in the sides of the recess first. This way, when the final panels are installed in the wall, the section of panel that borders on the alcove will lap over the end of the section that covers the alcove for a neater appearance.

You will cover all of this with compound and tape, at any rate, so it is not crucial if you install the sheetrock in another manner. When you fill in places below and above windows and above doors, try to have fitted edges of sheetrock meet where the fitting occurs.

If you will look at a panel of sheetrock you will see that the flat surface of the middle begins to taper slightly as you near the edge.

Now comes the tedious part of the work. When the sheetrock has been nailed up, you

need to tape and compound the joints and nail locations. It was suggested earlier that you should hit the nail head an extra time to make a dimple or sunken place in the sheetrock. The reason is obvious: if you leave the nail head even with the surface, you cannot cover the head without leaving a slight hump or raised place, which will be unsightly. It is also unsightly to leave the nail heads showing, so you make the small indentation and later you go back and fill the small depression with a putty-like compound.

You can buy the compound in five-gallon cans and get it cheaper than you could in smaller containers. The compound itself is soft and plastic, much like shortening or lard, when you buy it, but when you spread it over sections of the wall and it is exposed to heat and air for a few hours, it hardens to a plaster-like consistency. It never becomes hard like wood putty or mortar, and you can scratch it or chip it off even after it has hardened for months. Yet it is substantial enough that if you do not abuse it, it will last for decades.

You will need a putty knife and perhaps a trowel, depending upon the size of the expanse you need to putty. Start with the nail depressions. Open the can and you are ready to begin work. You need not mix or thin the compound. Dip the point of the putty knife into the compound and scoop up an amount the size of a small egg. Using a back-handed motion, spread the compound or putty across the depression.

Use a "feathering" motion as you spread the compound. Fill the depression and then thin the coating of compound more and more as you move away from the depression, until you have a smooth and uniform surface that is elevated slightly above the level of the sheetrock surface.

Do all of the nail holes in the same fashion, except those that you are certain will be covered by molding or baseboards. When the compound has hardened and set, use two grades of sandpaper to smooth the work.

Start with a coarse paper and brush it lightly over the compound. Do not rub hard or you will destroy your work. When you have knocked down the peaks and worst irregularities, use the smooth sandpaper and gently rub until you have smoothed the entire nail area so that it is as smooth and even as the rest of the sheetrock.

When you compound the joints, you may want to use tape under the compound. Some people prefer to apply a layer of compound, just as you did with the nail holes, and smooth it generally. Then they cut the appropriate length of special tape you can buy, and you push the tape down into the compound and then cover it with more compound.

This sounds like a lot, but you are really applying thin layers. You will apply only enough to fill the small sloped area at the edge of the panels. Actually you will over-fill the area slightly and then sand it down until it is on the same level as the rest of the panel.

Warning: wear a mask as you sand the compound. The fine dust will fill the air and you will inhale a considerable amount of it. The dust can irritate sinuses, trigger allergies, and cause bronchial congestion.

You will now see why it was suggested earlier that you try to fill smaller spaces with the factory-edged sections of sheetrock panels. If you use a full thickness, rather than the bevel types of edges, you will find that the compound and tape will cause an elevation that is an eyesore.

Sheetrock is a useful and tasteful way to cover walls and ceilings, but you will see, after you have worked with it for a while, that even though you can cover 32 square feet with each panel, and while it appears that the work is moving ahead at a rapid pace, you will still have hours and hours of compounding and sanding work ahead of you.

Whatever you choose to install is fine, as long as you are pleased, but ceiling tiles are usually easier to install and there is no follow-up work. The cost is close to the same.

If you choose to install knotty pine or similar wood, you will find that the cost is a little greater, but the finished product is superb. It takes a little longer to install the wood boards, but when you are finished, the job is done. You need not even paint the wood unless you want a special color. Knotty pine and oak are among the woods that are so attractive in their natural state that they need no embellishments.

But for the person who wants sheetrock, you will find that in spite of the amount of time and energy required, the finished product is as economical as any type of wall and ceiling covering you can find.

One suggestion is that you complete all of the work of hanging or nailing up the sheetrock before you start on the jointing and sanding, unless you must rig up a special work arrangement. For instance, if you must set up a scaffold or a temporary floor, as we had to do, it is easier to complete all of the work that must be done on the scaffold while it is in the original location.

When you must fit special pieces into areas over doors, for example, be sure to save the remainder of the panel. You will find that you must have small pieces for later work.

Incidentally, when you are taping and jointing and sanding, you will find that on corners it is easier to buy and install the lightweight angled and perforated metal. It is easier to push the metal into the compound and let the compound work its way through the perforations than it is to use tape.

Your only problem areas in the entire sheetrock work will likely come around light switches, receptacles, and fixtures. If you can do so, work out the panel so that one edge of it abuts the receptacle box or switch box or light fixture. You can measure the distance from the edge of the last panel installed to the edge of the electric box and then measure the sheetrock panel and cut accordingly, but if your estimates are off by an inch or so, you have an unsightly mess to tidy. If the box is to be on the edge of the panel, you can hold the panel in place and mark exactly where the cuts must be made.

Assume that you are installing sheetrock over-head and you have a light fixture in the center of the room. Take down the fixture first (after dealing with the power to the fixture), but even before you make this step, look over the problem. Can you, for instance, start a panel at the edge of the fixture and work backward to the wall? Can you do this on both sides? If you can, you can cut out half of the space needed for the fixture from one panel and the other half from the second panel. Then the two panels should fit neatly around the fixture.

But if you install the panel at the fixture after the other panels are already installed, you will have to measure with great precision and cut the same way. If you err, you may have ruined the entire panel.

On the topic of ceilings, you may find that the house you bought and moved has the old-fashioned high ceilings that make the house almost impossible to heat. If this is the case, you may want to lower the ceilings. If you wish to do this, the following chapter will offer suggestions on how to lower a ceiling without losing the strength and integrity of the original ceiling.

# Chapter Eighteen
# Lowering Ceilings

Imagine a huge cube that is 15 feet long, 15 feet wide, and 12 feet high. The total cubic feet (15 x 15 x 12) are 2,700. Now reduce that cube to 15 feet by 15 feet by 10 feet, and you have 2,250 cubic feet.

Take the cube down two more feet to 15 feet by 15 feet by 8, and you get 1,800 cubic feet. Now what does all this have to do with moving a house and restoring it?

The answer is that if the rooms in the house are modest in size (15 feet by 15 feet) and the ceilings are 12 feet high, you have 2,700 cubic feet of air to heat or cool. If you lower the ceiling to 10 feet you have eliminated 450 cubic feet, and if you lower the ceiling to a more traditional eight feet, you have now reduced the cubic footage by 900.

You have in effect reduced the cubic feet by about 35 per cent, which means, actually, more than a 35 percent savings on heating costs. The reason it is more than the mathematical 35 percent (roughly) is that heat, of course, rises, and the greatest amount of your heat will be against the ceiling where it will benefit no one, unless you have pro basketball players as house guests.

You will have a room that is uncomfortably cool at the floor to waist level and uncomfort-ably hot over your head. By lowering the ceiling in the room and saving almost 35 per cent of the cost of heating, you improve your comfort and finances at the same time.

Carry the idea one step beyond: If you lower the ceiling in several rooms, you will cut heating and cooling costs dramatically at a fairly low cost. If you need to do repair work on the ceiling of a room anyhow, this is a good reason to lower it and your heating bill at the same time.

Some people like high ceilings and don't mind living with the problems associated with them. I am a high-ceiling lover, and in the living room-den area of our house the cathedral ceiling is 24 feet high. There are advantages to the high ceiling where we live because we have more warm months than cold months, and the floor level is comfortably cool in the hottest part of the summer because much of the heat rises to the upper levels.

But in other parts of the house we have stuck with the more traditional ceiling heights, so we have the best of both worlds. High ceilings have beauty and grace, more so than low-ceilinged rooms.

Essentially it is a matter of taste. If you want lower ceilings, you can have them with only a small amount of trouble.

First, there are three basic ways of lowering a ceiling at a low cost. The most awkward and inefficient way, to me, is the most simple method. If the ceiling is 12 feet and you want it lowered to 10 feet, simply measure down from the ceiling while you stand on a ladder in one corner of the room. Mark the 10 foot height and then move to the other corner of that wall and repeat the measuring process. Then strike a chalk line from one mark to the other and you will have the first ceiling wall line.

Do the same at all four walls. When you mark the chalk line, you can drive a very small nail into the wood or sheetrock or plaster and loop the end of the chalk line over the nail. Then move to the other corner and pull the chalk line taut, then lift the line and snap it against the wall.

Mark all four walls. Now locate studs and mark these so that you can see to nail easily. Then secure long 2 x 4s and position them so that the bottom of the timber is aligned with the chalk line. Nail the 2 x 4 to the studs.

Install 2 x 4s completely around the room. When this is done, you will need to install girders, which can also be 2 x 4 timbers. These must be long enough to reach across the entire room so that you can nail them to the wall-mounted 2 x 4s. Nail up the girders so that they are spaced 16 inches on center.

You are now ready to nail tongue-and-groove lumber, sheetrock, or other types of ceiling coverings to the bottoms of the girders. If you elect to install ceiling tiles, you will need to nail up the wood strips — the nailers — as you did before.

The problem with this type of construction is that there is no support at all in the middle of the room. In time the girders may start to sag in the middle and create an unsightly problem.

You also have the problem of the cost of such long timbers. A 15-foot 2 x 4 may also be harder to find.

There are two basic aids for you relative to this problem. First, and this is not highly recommended, you can splice the 2 x 4s. To do so, lay two lengths of 2 x 4 on a work surface. Stand the timbers on edge and butt them end-to-end. Then nail a three-foot section of 1 x 4 board or plywood to both sides of the timber. This splice will support a great deal of weight and will resist sagging well.

A second method also involves plywood. If you install the 15-foot timbers, cut four-inch strips (actually 3.5-inch strips) and nail these to the sides of the timbers. The plywood will keep the girders from sagging.

A second (and better, if more costly) method of lowering the ceiling is to buy and install tracks that can be installed easily. You then simply lay ceiling tiles in place inside the tracks. You need not nail or staple or in any other way fasten the tiles. You can remove the tiles easily at any time you desire and you will not damage the tiles. Ask your local building-supplies dealer for the materials needed for this method.

A third method is more work but is very strong, durable, and attractive. In order to install this type of ceiling, you must first take down the existing ceiling. If the ceiling is of plaster, you will have a dusty mess. If the ceiling is sheetrock, the work is somewhat easier. If the ceiling is lightweight tiles, the job is no problem at all.

When the old ceiling is down, cut lengths of 2 x 4 that are as long as the amount you wish to lower the ceiling plus 3.5 inches. In other words, if you want to lower the ceiling by four feet, your 2 x 4 lengths need to be 4 feet plus 3.5 inches.

Start in one corner and nail the first 2 x 4 length to the joist. The 2 x 4 will hang down into the room four feet and will be snug against the wall in the corner. Assume that the room is 15 feet long and wide. You can nail the next length of 2 x 4 eight feet away, and the third one will be nailed in the corner.

Then locate an eight-foot 2 x 4 and nail it from the first corner to the second 2 x 4. The eight-foot 2 x 4 should be so positioned that it is flush with the bottom of the 2 x 4s along the joist.

Do the same with every joist. When you are finished, you will have a network of 2 x 4s to which you can nail up the sheetrock or other ceiling materials.

Use a level often and make certain that the new hanging joists are level all around the room. Remember that if you have one of the 2 x 4s slightly longer or shorter than it should be, you will have a very noticeable problem in your new ceiling. And you cannot correct it except by taking down the ceiling covering and either sawing off the too-long member or taking down the too short one and replacing it with another. This is a great deal of unnecessary work that is also costly in terms of materials and your time.

Here is an inexpensive method of improving the room even more while you are working on the ceiling. As soon as you put up one course of ceiling cover, pause and lay batts of insulation between the hanging joists. Each time you complete a course, do the same. When you come to the last course, after each panel of sheetrock measure and cut sections of insulation from a batt and lay the sections atop the sheetrock.

The insulation costs little, comparatively speaking, and you will, particularly if this is an upstairs room, save a great deal more on heating and cooling bills. Even if it is a downstairs room (in a one-story house), you can do the same thing. You will create a dead-air space which makes the heating and cooling jobs much easier.

There are other times when it is necessary or highly desirable to lower entire ceilings, but there are also times when lowering only a part of a ceiling is important. If you have done extra plumbing, such as adding a new bath or expanding an older half-bath to install a tub and shower, for instance, you may have a problem concerning what to do with the pipes that must now be run along the ceiling of a basement room or down the wall of an adjacent room.

If the pipes must be run along the ceiling, it is best to install them near a wall. Now you can take down one course of ceiling covering and again cut 2 x 4 lengths to drop down from the

ceiling only enough to cover the pipes. It is likely that the pipes will be no more than a foot below the ceiling and often they are less than that. In such a case, drop a 2 x 4 from the joists and then run a third 2 x 4 across the bottom of the two hanging 2 x 4s.

Notice that in Figure 18-1 the pipes are high enough that they almost touch the joists. Right below the pipes are the 2 x 4s that are hanging from the short lengths of lumber that were nailed to the joists (not visible in this photo). You can see the sheetrock attached to the 2 x 4s.

**Figure 18-1**
*Section of lowered ceiling.*

The hanging timbers could be only one foot long or even shorter. Do this all along the wall, and then cover the framing of the new ceiling. You can cut a panel of sheetrock into several smaller pieces that will cover the framework and cost you very little money while you are doing it.

If you have a basement, you obviously had to install duct work if you have a heating system.

The duct work is unsightly, as it runs across ceilings and along walls in the basement. You can solve the problem in part by modifying the earlier suggestions about building the framework.

You need not run the ceiling framework along the entire room. You can take down the ceiling covering adjacent to the duct work, or, if the heating system has just been installed, there will not be any ceiling covering at all and you can frame around the ducts and then install the ceiling as suggested earlier.

Go to the duct area and again nail up the 2 x 4s that hang down from the joists. Possibly the duct is taken through a wall, and you need to enclose only three or four feet of it. Install the hanging 2 x 4s and as before run the hanging joist lengths by nailing them flush with the ends of the hanging 2 x 4s. Then cover the framework with whatever materials you plan to use in the remainder of the basement or room. Figure 18-2 shows a duct area that is covered by lowering the ceiling in that area only. Sheetrock has been installed to cover the framing of the lowered ceiling.

The same basic principles described above apply to any part of a ceiling that needs to be lowered. If the plumbing pipes run across one part of the basement, for instance, you can box in that portion of the basement and install sheetrock or other material to cover the framework.

Assume that your basement plumbing lines run along the wall of the house, essentially the full length, and that the pipes are three or four feet from the wall. Rather than boxing in the pipes and having the recessed area against the wall, box in the entire three- or four-foot area.

Go to the first joist and measure out, for example, four feet and mark the point. Then drive a small nail in half an inch at the spot. Now go to the other end of the basement and again measure out four feet. Mark the point.

Then loop the end of the chalk line over the nail head and pull the line the entire length of the basement. Strike the chalk line and you will have the location of all the hangers you need to install. As before, cut your lengths from 2 x 4 timbers. If you plan to drop the wall a foot, the hangers should be one foot plus the height of the joist. If you have ten-inch joists, you will need 22-inch hangers.

You will need to install the hangers against the wall and at the four-foot mark. As you did before, when you have the hangers in place so that one end butts against the subflooring, nail them securely, and then when all hangers are nailed in place, cut 2 x 4 lengths to reach from the outside edges of both hangers on the sides of the plumbing pipes.

If your basic length is four feet, you need 49 inches for each cross timber plus 3.5 inches to allow for the width of each of the 2 x

**Figure 18-2**
*Duct area framed in by lowering ceiling.*

4s, thus making your entire cross timber 55 inches long. Cut and install the cross timbers.

You will notice when you try to nail the cross timber at the first end that the bottom end of the 2 x 4 hanger will give back and forth and make nailing difficult. One help is to lay the cross timber on a work surface and, after you have marked the nail locations, drive the nails until the points barely stick through the other side.

When you put the cross timber up, use the C-clamp to hold the cross timber tightly against the hanger. If you have two clamps, use one on each side so that the cross timber is supported well. Now reach behind the cross timber and hanger and hold the hanger as you hit the nails. Your hand will help to stabilize the hanger, and although there will be some giving, you can drive the nails. When you have one nail completely driven, go to the other side and drive one nail. Then take the clamps down so you have more nailing room.

It is a good idea to nail the cross timber to the first and second hangers on one side at first. When both sides are done, then nail the cross timber across the ends. If the end hangers are flush against the basement wall, you will need to cut the cross timber short and fit it between the hangers.

Do not close in the clean-out at the end of the large drain pipe. This clean-out is there for one purpose: If you ever have stopped-up plumbing, you can run a clean-out rod or a plumber's "snake" down the pipe and dislodge the debris. The clean-out end of the pipe should be far enough from the wall that you can get the snake into the end of the pipe.

If you feel the need to cover the end of the lowered ceiling, use materials that can be taken down easily. If you use sheetrock, do not compound and tape unless you need the neater and more finished look. A neat fit will suffice, particularly since few people will see the work. An even better idea is to install a small access door so that you can simply remove or open the access door in order to reach the clean-out.

To install an access door, run two extra hangers a foot or so apart so that the clean-out is between the two hangers, which will serve as the rough opening for the door. Now cut a square or rectangle of plywood that will fit inside the rough opening. Use small hinges and a hook and eyelet to hold the door in place until you need to open it.

The next chapter deals with one of the final problems you will face with your new house: Leveling any areas in need.

# Chapter Nineteen
# Final Leveling Procedures

Earlier it was stated in this book that when a house is moved the mover will actually level the house better than it was when it was in its original setting. This does not mean that the house will be perfectly level. Anyone who has ever tried to level a small building project knows that at times it is very difficult to secure a perfectly level reading.

But many houses still on their original sites are not level, as a walk through them will demonstrate. If you examine the photo in Figure 19-1 you will see several obvious problems, yet this house was moved and the problems were corrected.

If you have laid masonry block, for instance, you know that the beginner has difficulty in leveling just one block in a wall. If you level the block from front to back, then one corner

may dip or rise and the side-to-side level reading is off. Keeping an entire wall level is a real challenge unless you are experienced as a mason.

**Figure 19-1**
*A house in trouble can be improved during moving.*

Now imagine the problems encountered in attempting to level an entire house. Go into any house that has been standing for a few years and place a level on the floors of the different rooms and then hold the level against the walls. It is a rare house that has retained its level position over the years.

**Figure 19-2**
*Preparing a place to set up a jack to raise corners.*

For that matter it is a rare house that is perfectly level and square even when it has just been completed. So you face a real test of your abilities when you set out to level the entire house from front to back.

First, though, what is wrong with having a floor that is half a bubble off level? For one thing, the fact that a floor has dropped slightly in the center tells you that, probably, the floor joists are starting to sag. This may mean that the joists were installed when they contained too much moisture content. In other words, they were green. They had not been properly dried. Or they contain only sap wood that has no real integrity when it comes to holding power and sustaining heavy weights.

The sagging may also mean that the joists were spaced too far apart and are inadequate to support the load that has been placed upon them. Sagging may also mean that the joists were too small to do the job.

When we were engaged in a building project we ordered a load of 2 x 12 timbers, several hundred of them, and when the load arrived I pointed out to the driver that the timbers were not 2 x 12s. He insisted that they were, that I should realize that a 2 x 12 is only a nominal size, and that after dressing, the timbers were intended to be only about 1.5 inches thick and 11.5 inches wide.

I finally took a tape measure to the timbers and showed him that the timbers were 2 x 8s, not 2 x 12s. At this point the driver called the main office and they informed him that I could simply double the timbers and get the same holding power I'd get from a 2 x 12. The office also said that a 2 x 8 was sufficient to support the weight of a rather large house.

To be brief, I told the man at the office not to urinate on my leg and try to convince me that it was raining. I further suggested that I was sending the entire load back and that they should store it where there was no danger of the sun's blistering the wood.

I mention this unsavory story only to point out that when your new house was built, someone may have used timbers too light for the job, and you now have a sagging floor. The sagging, as I indicated earlier, is not terrible in its own right, but the problem is that the sagging is indicative of other and more serious problems.

Another reason for sagging may be that the span covered by the joists was too great. This is common in many older houses.

You can correct the problem of sagging joists in one of three or four basic ways. First, buy a small, medium-duty hydraulic jack, one of the types that you can set on a solid base and pump up so that it will lift astonishing weights — up to about 8,000 pounds, depending upon the type of jack you buy.

Crawl under the house and use a shovel to scoop out dirt until you have a basically level work area of about two square feet. This area should be directly between two sagging joists and at the worst part of the problem. See Figure 19-2.

Build yourself a solid base for the jack to sit on. Such a base may be made of thick oak timbers two feet or so long. You can also use cement blocks if you will place a short but thick section of a timber across the cores of the block. Use nothing less than a 2 x 10 section. Be sure, too, that the jack will be lifting at a point that is stable and sturdy. Repair any obvious problems. See Figure 19-3.

Build up the base until the top of the jack at its lowest setting is six inches below the joists. Insert the jack handle and be ready to start pumping. Before you do, locate a strong and thick section of timber, preferably a six-by-six inch length, and set this section on top of the jack so that the ends of the timber are under two joists and you have three or four good inches sticking out on each side of the joists.

Now start to pump, slowly. You can see the cement blocks start to sink into the dirt at first, and when the blocks have compressed the dirt tightly you will see the joists begin to rise very slowly.

Do not get in a rush. You are under a house that you are lifting (at least you are lifting a part of it), and your insurance agent and OSHA would scream in terror. Do not think for a moment that this is a totally safe operation, but at the same time if the jack slips, the house is not going to collapse and bury you under it. If such a slight jolt would destroy your house, you wouldn't want to live it in anyway.

When you have raised the joist until it is level again, you can hold the joist in that position in a couple of ways. First, you can "scab" a second joist to the original one. Hold the joist in place and use 16d nails, three in a row, every 18 inches. When you have completed the nailing, the joist should be level and it should remain that way.

**Figure 19-3**
*Making corrections prior to raising corner.*

You can also build a new pillar or foundation pier at the sagging area. Keep the joist jacked up while you gather cement blocks and/or bricks and pour a concrete footing and then build the pier. If your blocks or bricks do not come out exactly right at the top, you can slip short lengths of oak boards between the bottom of the joist and the top of the pier.

When you are through, release the pressure on the jack very slowly and lower the jack and move to your next work spot. Do not release the pressure suddenly.

If the joists were spaced too far apart, your only answer is to install extra joists between the original ones. Again, you will need to jack up the joists, two at a time, as before, so that the floor is level. While the jack is holding the floor at the desired level, install the new joist between the sagging ones. You may need to install several joists in order to keep the floor level.

You may find that termite or other insect damage has so weakened the joists that they have started to give way. Your only solution here is to take out the joists and replace them with new ones.

To take out a series of joists, you should remove only one at a time and then replace it before you remove any others. Go to each end and, using a pry bar or a three-pound hammer, loosen the ends of the joist and pull it out. Then stand the new joist in its place and nail it in.

Another problem that might create sagging is that bridging was omitted when the house was built. Bridging is the use of metal strips, wood strips, or short timbers to keep the joists from leaning sideways. Over the years the weight of the house may be great enough that the joists start to cave in slowly as they spread from the top to bottom, and as they spread, they allow the house to sink a little at a time.

If this is your problem, your solution is to add the bridging, whether metal strips or wood sections. The metal strips are easy to install under normal conditions. When the joists are in erect position, you simply position one of the metal bridges so that one end rests upon the top of one joist and fits at the bottom of the adjacent joist. Then you nail the bridging in place. At the same location you install the second bridging, but this time you do it from the opposite direction so that the two pieces create an X between the

joists. You install the bridging pairs every few feet along a joist.

But if your joists are starting to collapse, you cannot use the metal bridging. So you are left with the wood bridging.

Again, under ideal conditions, you would cut two lengths of boards or timbers and angle-cut them so that the two, when they are installed, make another X figure, with the bridging units placed side by side.

But you cannot use this method, either, if the joists are not in an erect position. The reason the two previous methods are mentioned is that if your joists are still in good shape you might want to install the bridging if none is present in your new house.

If you want to use the corrective measure, there is only one way that works effectively. This method involves the use of 2 x 12 or 2 x 10 timber sections that are about 14 inches long. The best dimension for the bridging is stock that is the same size as that of the joists. If your joists are 2 x 12, then use short lengths of 2 x 12 stock.

The lengths should be just long enough to fit inside or between the joists. If joists are spaced 16 inches on center then you will have about 14 inches between the joists. Measure to get the exact length and then cut the pieces for a perfect fit. If the bridging is too long, you cannot get it in place, and if it is too short, it will not hold effectively.

When you have the first bridging piece cut, wedge it into the space between joists as tightly as you can. The piece should form right angles with the joists, but if the joists are sinking you cannot get the bridging all the way in place.

At this point you use a hammer. With the bridging wedged in as far as you can get it, use a medium-weight hammer at the top of the bridging. Tap it further and further into the opening until the bridging forces the joists upward into a nearly erect position. Then tap along the center, first on one side and then on the other.

If you see that your bridging is splitting, stop and take the piece out. Locate a four-by-four section of timber and place it as close to the top of the joists as you can get it. Use a heavier hammer, a three-pounder, and bang the four-by-four into position. Then position your bridging piece in place and nail it in. Drive nails from the other side of the joists so that the nails pass through the joist and into the ends of the bridging.

Now take down the four-by-four. You may have to use a pry bar in order to extricate it from its wedged position. Move down the joist another six feet and install another bridging piece.

This may sound like a lot of trouble, but you in fact are preventing, not causing, trouble. When the bridging work is done, the joists should be back at their normal locations.

Not all sinking occurs in the center of the joists. Some of it, in fact, quite a lot of it, occurs at corners. Other sinking occurs along the outside walls where the foundation walls were built on inferior footings that were either too thin, composed of an unstable concrete mix, or built on soil that was bad. The footing could have been too shallow, not below the frost line, or the soil could have been too loose. Sometimes the masons will begin to lay blocks before the concrete has set up properly.

Whatever the reasons, the foundation wall area might be sinking, and if it is, when the house is moved you can make the corrections. First, be sure that your own foundation walls are built properly and on good footings. Let the footings settle and dry for at least 24 hours before you build foundation walls.

You will find that if an exterior wall has been allowed to remain in a sunken position for a long period of time, the timbers of the wall will have conformed to their new position and they will have dried and cured in that position. The only possible corrections are to force them back into the original position or to take them out and replace them.

First, if you have ever observed the effect of time on green wood, you know what happens. Assume that you have cut a green 1 x 5 board from a pine tree. You lay the board in a dry place and leave it. Within a matter of days the board will start to warp and bow. Within two weeks the board has assumed a totally new shape, and there is little that can be done about it other than to force it back to its original shape and hold it in that shape until it cures completely.

With your house, you may be able to use the jack to raise the timbers to their original conformation. First, build the foundation wall to within one course of the house walls. When the foundation wall has set up completely, place a wide and thick and strong section of timber across the wall blocks and then set the jack on the blocks and timber section. Use another wide and strong section of wood at the top of the jack.

Now pump the jack up until the wall levels. Check the floors inside for a level reading. When you are satisfied, return to the outside and build the foundation wall all the way to the top. You will have to leave out the section where the jack is located, at least for now. Let the foundation wall set up after it has been built up so that it touches the wall.

After a 24-hour wait, you can remove the supports that held the wall in place and then fill in the blocks you left out so the jack would have operating room. Your wall should be in good shape now and for many years to come.

If you need to take out joists or sills that are beyond repair, the time to do this is while the house is still on the steel. You can make many of the needed repairs to the house while it is still jacked up.

If one corner is too low, you will need to go under the house to a point near the corner and set up your jack assembly that consists of cement blocks, timber sections, and the top piece for the jack. Here, with the foundation wall in place, you set up the jack and pump it until the corner has been raised to the proper level. Then you can insert shims of metal or oak under the corner to hold the level position. A shim of the sort that you can use should be as wide as the foundation wall and three or four feet long.

**Figure 19-4**
*A house that has been leveled before foundation walls were built.*

**Figure 19-5**
*Installing braces and raising a roof corner.*

Sometimes the out-of-level situations occur with ceilings rather than with joists. In order to correct a sagging ceiling, you must set up a jack inside the house and raise the ceiling level to the desired point.

Here's how to do the work, and it is rather tricky. Locate a long, thick, and wide length of timber on which to set the jack. Locate another similar piece to place against the ceiling. Then locate a 4 x 4 or 6 x 6 timber long enough to reach from the jack to the ceiling, which means one seven feet long or longer, depending upon your ceiling height.

Have someone hold the timber atop the jack while you or someone else pumps up the jack until the top of the timber is within two inches of the ceiling. Now someone must climb a ladder or reach high enough to position the top piece of timber over the top of the 6 x 6 timber.

When the jack is pumped slightly higher, the top timber will be held in place by pressure. Keep pumping very slowly until the ceiling sag is removed. Then, with the jack assembly still in place, you must go to the attic and remove any plywood flooring or insulation in the way of your work, and then cut strips of plywood and nail these on both sides of the ceiling joists. The plywood should be at least half an inch thick and should be as wide as the joists are high. Use at least 16d nails to attach the plywood to the side of the joists. Use rows of nails spaced two feet apart. When you let the jack down, the ceiling will stay in place.

This procedure works inside or out. With the house off the ground and off the foundation wall, as shown in Figure 19-4, build piers, jack the house up to the desired level, and then lower the house onto the piers.

Using the same basic techniques, you can go throughout the house, under it as well as inside it, and look for any areas that are in need of leveling. With the hydraulic jack you can correct almost any part of the house that needs to be elevated slightly. Use the jack to raise the corners of car ports and then build the foundation walls, as shown in Figure 19-5. With the foundation wall in place and the roof level, install the corner posts, as shown in Figure 19-6, and you have saved yourself a lot of trouble in the immediate future.

The final chapter of this book is geared to discussing a wide range of topics. This chapter is a series of suggestions for correcting or improving small but important tasks.

**Figure 19-6**
*Corner posts installed and roof leveled.*

# Chapter Twenty
# Final Touches

One of the best investments you can make in a house is plenty of insulation. While the house does not have the foundation wall under it, you have a marvelous opportunity to install insulation underneath the house. You can crawl under the elevated structure and staple insulation between joists and help save money on heating and cooling.

Insulation, of course, does not make a house warmer or cooler; it simply prevents a house from getting cooler or warmer. That is, the insulation does not produce any heat at all. What it does is keep heated or cooled air from passing from outside the house to inside the house.

Another point: No amount of insulation will keep heat or cold from passing through it. All the insulation can do is slow down the rate at which the unwanted heat or cold penetrates the barrier.

When you install insulation, you will find instructions on each roll or package of insulation. Generally speaking, when you install insulation in walls between studs, you make certain that the vapor barrier faces the inside of the room. The vapor barrier is the paper backing on the insulation rolls. You will also find tabs that unfold from the paper. These tabs, which run the full length of the roll, will, if your studs are

spaced properly, fit over the edge of the studs, and the insulation itself will fit perfectly inside or between the studs.

With the tabs lapped over the stud edges, you can use a staple gun to fasten the tabs to the studs. This type of fastening will not resist rough treatment, but it will hold until you can get the wall coverings installed. Once the insulation is in place, protect the vapor barrier to keep it from being torn or ripped.

When you work on insulation, be sure to wear long-sleeved shirts and long pants. Eye protection is a must. The tiny fibers which float in the air as you work can wreck your bronchial system, and I have always found it crucial to wear a mask of some type. The fibers which irritate bronchial tubes can also be a bad irritant of eyes and skin, and you will find that your eyes water and your flesh stings and itches unless you wear protective clothing.

If the job will take more than one day, be sure to lay the clothing you wore while working aside and wash these separate from other clothes. You may want to wear the same clothes for two days or so, until the job is completed, rather than contaminating other clothes.

If the job can be done in two or three hours, it is good to have a change of clothing handy so you won't have to wear the same clothing for other work.

When you are filling in between studs, if the studs are not spaced properly you will need to make adjustments in your work. If the studs are too wide, you can use the tab to fasten one side, but the other side will hang loose. So measure the distance remaining inside the stud space and cut strips of insulation from a section from the roll. Always cut the strip slightly longer and wider than you need it. For instance, if the space is six inches, cut the strip eight inches.

**Figure 20-1**
*Insulation installation.*

An easy way to cut insulation is with a regular pair of household scissors. When you cut the strips, push it gently into the space and use the tab on one side of the strip. The outward pressure of the insulation will serve to keep it inside the studs while you complete the job. You

can also use Scotch tape or masking tape across the place where the sections of insulation meet. Half a dozen strips six inches long will suffice.

If you have the window and door facings or trim down, you will possibly see an open space between window and door and the rough frame. Cut small strips of insulation and install it in the space. If you have not had this experience before, you will be astounded at the amount of cold air that can come through a tiny hole. Even the space around light switches and boxes can admit a shocking amount of cold air. See Figure 20-1 for an example of how much space there can be between windows or around window frames. While this house was extremely well-built, there is no way to keep all the crevices closed during construction.

**Figure 20-2**
*Repairing walls and installing insulation.*

With wall coverings down, or with studding only partially exposed, you can install a great deal of insulation, as you see in Figure 20-2.

You can even get in some quality time with the family members.

When you put in the insulation pieces, do not pack or compress them into the space. The effectiveness of insulation is based on the fact that the dead-air space deters the passage of cold or hot air, and if you pack the insulation in, you will shut down the dead-air spaces and reduce greatly the effectiveness of insulation.

If you plan to do any painting, a good time would be while you have the window and door trim down. You may want to use a flat paint on the walls and a semi-gloss paint on windows, doors, molding, and baseboards. While these units of wood are down, paint them and let them dry in a safe place. Then after the walls are painted, install the trim and molding. By doing the work in this manner you eliminate the smears of unwanted paint on the wrong places.

This is elementary, but use a drop cloth under all paint jobs. Do not let green paint stain the beautiful oak flooring. Carry a small cloth in your pocket as you work, and if you let a drop of paint fall, clean it up then and there. The longer you wait, the harder the job will be.

If you are painting outside, be sure to wait until the wood is totally dry. If the wood is wet, the paint will trap droplets of water and the heat of the sun will pull this moisture from the wood and cause the paint to bubble, chip, and crack. Be sure to scrape old paint from the surface you plan to paint. Do not paint over flaking paint.

If you want to go in the other direction and remove paint rather than apply it, the job can be a difficult one. You can scrape it off and brush it off by using a putty knife or a steel-wire brush, but these are effective primarily when the paint is loose and flaking. If you must take off a prime coat of enamel, you can try using three grades of sandpaper. Start with a coarse paper and wrap the paper over a block of wood. Holding the block tightly, scrub the paper back and forth until the paint turns to powder. Then use a medium grade of sandpaper and clear off as much of the remaining paint as you can. Finish

up with a fine grade of paper to eliminate any scratch marks made by the other sandpaper.

If you must clean paint out of corners, use the corner of the block and push the block up and down until the paper rips away the paint. If this doesn't work, you can try some of the paint strippers available on the market. You can apply the remover with a brush and wait a few minutes for it to cut through the paint, and then you can use a putty knife to remove the majority of the rest of the paint.

There is another way that works fairly well that I use whenever I must remove stubborn paint. I buy one of the electric drill attachments and use it. You can get wire brush attachments, and when you use them, simply install them into the drill and then hold the drill parallel with the ground and let the bristles remove the paint. The bristles will reach down into shallow crevices and into corners and remove paint that sandpaper cannot reach. The brushes are inexpensive, but you will use several of them on a big job. Their best uses are for cleaning paint away from doors, windows, and wooden door and window frames.

When your house has been moved, you may find that some of the doors and windows are extremely tight. This tightness does not necessarily result from the moving; perhaps the window has been stuck for years, or the door has tended to stick during wet weather since the house was built.

You can correct these problems or at least improve them in a variety of ways. To keep the door from sticking, push the door gently closed and observe carefully to see where the door does not fit inside the frame well. Then use a rasp if the problem is small. The rasps can be bought in a variety of forms, but my own favorite is the one with the handle on one end and the knob on the other. The metal shape of the rasp is that of an elongated rectangle, and the bottom of it is like a grater for vegetables. If you grasp the knob in one hand and the handle in the other and then push down gently and move the rasp back and forth with a slow and steady motion, you can shave off the right amount of wood to allow the door to open and close easily.

If the rasp cannot do the job, you might want to try a hand-held plane or planer. Set the blade at its most shallow point and, starting at the lowest point that needs shaving on the door, push up toward the top of the door and let the blade of the planer bite into the wood. Be careful that you do not let the blade dig too deeply or you will mar the edge of the door badly.

Stuck windows are another matter. You cannot get any type of instrument to the problem unless you take the window apart. You can try two methods that usually work fairly well. The first is the simplest. Use the heel of your hand and bump the window stile or side unit of wood. Several solid bumps will likely break loose the paint that has welded the wood of the window to the wood of the frame.

If this doesn't work, try squirting penetrating oil down along the window stile and allow a few minutes for the oil to create a lubricating effect. The window may open and close properly after ten minutes.

Another possible solution is to remove the stool (the wide length of board that is parallel to the ground and fits into the window frame flat. There are other names applied to this part of the window, so don't be confused if you hear alternative labels.). The edge of the stool butts into the bottom rail of the window sash. You may have to remove the apron (the board installed just under the stool) before you can remove the stool.

When you can do it, work the blade of a small pry bar into the crack between the window frame bottom and the rail or bottom piece of the window sash. Pry gently until the window breaks free and moves slightly up and down. Do not pry hard or you will exert such pressure on the window that you will crack the panes. As soon as the window sash breaks free, push it back down, and then pull it up again. Keep working the sash up and down until it moves freely. Then

apply a thin coating of penetrating oil or grease, not enough to soil the wood noticeably but only enough to provide lubrication.

You may find that the screws in a door hinge are loose and they will not tighten because the wood inside the door frame or jamb has been ground away until there are no fibers left to exert pressure on the screws. You can correct this problem in most instances with a matchstick — from one of the old wooden matches.

Remove the screw and then push the bare end of the match into the hole as far as it will go. When the matchstick hits the bottom of the hole, break it off inside the hole. Then use a screwdriver to sink the screw again. The wood of the matchstick will provide the needed fibers to give the screw holding power.

If window trim has deteriorated over the years and you wish to replace it, here's a simple way to do so. Take the old trim down carefully and then measure the stool of the window. You can even mark the new wood by laying the old atop the new and marking around it. Saw out the unwanted wood and install the stool exactly as it was when the old trim was in place.

Now mark, cut, and install the apron directly under the stool. Mark and cut the side trim and install it. You can see the imprint left by the old trim and you can let the new wood conform to the old position. Mark and cut the top of the trim and then mark the new wood exactly the same length as the old. Saw and install the trim top. The window is now complete.

If the old trim is missing, you can still do the work with little difficulty. Pull down the window and cut the stool wood and hold it in position. Mark where the window frame and the stool unit meet. Be sure to mark both sides.

Let the ends of the stool extend past the point where you will want to cut them later. Now measure from the inside edge of the window rail at the bottom to the outside edge of the stool wood. Note the distance, then measure over that exact distance from the outside edge of the stool to the corresponding distance from the window rail to the stool edge.

You may find that the distance is not exactly the same on both sides of the window. This discrepancy likely resulted from the fact that the window was originally installed incorrectly a fraction of an inch, but it is not a serious matter. Few if any people would notice a sixteenth of an inch deviation.

But you should cut the stool exactly according to the correct measurements. If you do not, the wood will not seat against the window sash properly and will admit cold or hot air and let your own cooling or heating escape.

Nail the stool to the window framing and then cut and install the apron. The apron should align with the stool in length. You now need to cut the side trim units. You have two basic ways in which to cut the material. You can use a square corner or a mitered corner at the top, and you can install the side trim first and fit the top to it, or you can install the top and fit the side trim to it.

If you want a square trim, you will need to measure from the top of the stool to the top of the window assembly. Keep in mind that the side trim should cover the window framing and should align with it exactly, and the top trim should likewise cover and align with the framing. So measure to the exact bottom of the framing and then measure and cut stock, usually 1 x 4 boards one inch or three-fourths inch thick. Your thickness needs to be such that the outside edge will look right with the size of window you have. A much larger window, for instance, might look far better with a wider trim board.

When the stock is cut, use finish nails to install it. Then lay a piece of stock across the tops of both side trim boards and mark the outside points of the side trim as it fits against the bottom edge of the top trim. Mark both sides, cut along the lines, and install, and the window is essentially complete.

If you want mitered corners, you can handle the work in the following manner. First, a mitered corner is one that has two angles that fit together perfectly. The top trim is mitered from the outside and upper corner down to the top corner of the window framing. The side trim is mitered from the top corner down to the window framing. When the two angles meet, they form a neat and perfect alignment.

To match the mitered corners, you must mark and cut with care. Otherwise you will have a gap at one or both corners. Start by cutting the side trim at a 45-degree angle. To get the perfect cut, measure the width of the board. Take the exact width of the board and measure that distance down from the top end of the board.

If the board is six inches wide, measure down exactly six inches and mark the point. Use a square to draw a line straight across the board at that distance. You have now a perfect square formed by the part of the board from the line to the end of the board. Now lay the square or any other straight edge diagonally across the square and mark along the straight edge from the outside top corner to the inside bottom corner of the square. Cut along the line and lay the triangle aside. Do the same on the other board.

You can now mark the top trim board in one of two ways. The first way is to use the triangle you cut from each side and lay the triangle against the end of the board so that the triangle aligns with the top of the board and the point is at the bottom of the board. There will be a triangle of space at the end of the board. The triangle will not be covered by the first triangle.

Mark along the line and cut off the triangle. Do this on both ends, and when you install the side trim and it is nailed in place, the top trim unit should fit perfectly into the angled corners.

If you want to be doubly sure of your angles, nail up the side trim but do not sink the nails completely. Leave the board out from the window at the top far enough that the top trim board will slip behind the side boards.

Now slip the top trim board behind the two side trim pieces. Be sure that the top edge of the top trim board is aligned exactly with the outside edge of the side trim board. With the top trim unit held securely in place, mark along the slope of the side trim board onto the top trim piece. Do this on both sides, and then cut along the lines. The top trim will not fit perfectly to form angled corners.

You may find that over the years some of the wall covering has, because of house settling, moved away from the door or window trim. If you put in new sheetrock, for instance, fill the space, if any, between the edge of the panel and the door frame with compound, allow it to harden, and then sand it. Figure 20-3 shows the correction of door and wall covering problems.

**Figure 20-3**
*Dealing with sheet rock and door frames.*

You may, after the house is moved, decide to replace floor and ceiling molding, especially if some of the existing molding had been damaged slightly. You will find that molding is extremely expensive on a per-foot basis, and molding for one room or for a hallway can be highly expensive, so you are advised to retain the original molding if it is serviceable.

If a length of molding is cracked or unsightly, you can help to solve the problem by carefully

taking up the entire length of molding first. Use a thin-bladed pry bar slipped under the molding in a corner or other area where any scratches you make will not be highly visible. If a couch, for instance, is to occupy the wall, make the repairs so that they will be hidden by the couch.

When you start to remove the molding, elevate a section of it an inch or less, and then slip another pry bar, claws of a hammer, or blade of a heavy screwdriver underneath it. Use a small piece of wood as a fulcrum to make the prying upward easier. Take great care not to crack the molding. If you hear the unmistakable sound of wood cracking, stop applying pressure at once. Move to another area, and try to pry as close to the nails as possible.

When you can do so, work your way to one end of the molding and free one end. Do not try to pull up the remainder of the length. You are highly likely to break the piece. Instead, hold the free section in one hand so that there is slight pressure on the length. Then with the other hand use a pry bar to urge gently on the still-nailed section. You can remove the entire section in this manner and do little if any damage.

When the previously damaged section is out, cut out the shortest possible section with the damage in it. Then take the section to the building supply house to try to match it from their stock. Buy as little as possible — the exact length or slightly more than the sample you took to the store.

Cut the section straight across so that it fits the empty space. If you bought the exact length needed, you need not worry about cutting. Place the section into position and use small finish nails to install it.

**Figure 20-4**
*Putting up storm windows.*

Cut the section with a hand saw to avoid splintering, and nail the new section in place.

If there is a noticeable gap, use wood putty or make your own mixture of sawdust and glue. Use a putty knife to pack the mixture into the gap. Let the mixture dry and then sand it until it conforms to the shape of the original molding. Then paint or stain the entire molding, and the repair work will be barely noticeable.

Before you move in, you may wish to install storm windows to cut heat and cooling losses greatly. You can also install siding around windows and doors, if you have a brick house and you wish to eliminate painting chores later. Figures 20-4 shows installation of storm windows, and Figure 20-5 shows the mounting of shutters to give the windows a dressier look.

If the piece to be replaced reached to a corner, you will need to make a corner cut, which can be very difficult. The best method for making the corner cut is, if you can do so without great difficulty, to take up the molding from the wall that forms the corner. Then lay the new piece down so that the squared end extends into the corner. Now push the second piece up against the new section and mark along the solid piece and onto the new piece. Remove the full-length piece and lay it aside for the moment and install the new length. Then re-install the second piece you took up.

This method works for either ceiling molding or floor molding. However, with ceiling molding you cannot hide the repair work as well as you can with floor molding. Your best bet is to buy a full length of molding and replace the entire section. If this proves to be more expensive than you wish, take down the damaged section, cut out the bad spot, and buy a length to replace it.

**Figure 20-5**
*Adding shutters and a touch of taste to the house.*

When you are building foundation walls, don't forget to leave space for venting. Figure 20-6 shows a vent hole left between the brick foundation wall and the house wall framing.

**Figure 20-6**
*Vent opening in foundation wall.*

More brief suggestions: If you must take the upper floor of the house apart, or if you had to take down the chimney, this is a fine time to introduce into the house items that would be very difficult to negotiate otherwise. Figure 20-7 shows one way to get a bathtub unit upstairs in the most convenient manner.

This book will not attempt to tell you how to build a good chimney, for two reasons: space and the author's ignorance. We hired a professional mason to do the starting work, including the draft and fireplace, and then, as he told

us, anyone can stack bricks from that point on. I will not pretend that I felt very comfortable atop the rickety scaffold; I was terrified, but the thought of saving hundreds of dollars motivated us to climb that scaffold and do the best job we could. The chimney shown in Figure 20-8 worked with astonishing effectiveness.

After the house is moved, if you had to dismantle part of it, you will feel that it will never go back together again. You are disgusted with leaks and rattling window panes. Now is the time to find the courage to climb to the rooftop and make the necessary shingle repairs — before you move furniture into the house. Figure 20-9 shows a courageous woman doing her best work. Women, I guarantee you, can do any kind of construction work.

We found that for soundproofing and extra insulation we could put up sheetrock plus paneling. We had a very good buy on both and decided to invest in the extra stability. So we put up the sheetrock and compounded the joints, but we did not feather and sand. Figure 20-10 shows the beginning of the paneling work and Figure 20-11 shows the reward of the work. The chimney and fireplace were both built with salvaged brick.

**Figure 20-7**
*Taking bathtub unit into the house the easy way.*

**Figure 20-8**
*Completing the chimney work.*

**Figure 20-10**
*Starting the paneling and insulation work.*

**Figure 20-9**
*Last-minute roof repair work.*

**Figure 20-11**
*The reward of the work.*

**Figure 20-12 and 20-13**
*Houses to go — for a song!*

You can follow the basic suggestions given in this book to correct other problems encountered. These will be minor in nature under nearly all circumstances. Follow the basic principles of carpentry described here, and you can handle the work easily.

Best of all, you will get one of the greatest deals in the history of housing. You have perhaps heard others insist that the day of terrific deals on anything are gone, but if you find a good, sound, and easy-to-move house, you can buy the structure, hire someone to move it, and do the restoration work yourself.

Your finished product will cost you less than one-fourth what you might normally expect to pay for a traditional house on the market today. In our own case, we bought the house, had it moved, and restored it for far less than the price of a used late-model automobile, and we believed then, and we believe now, that the bargain was a wonderful one.

I wish you the same success with your own ventures. Take another look at the houses in Figures 20-12 and 20-13 moving to new locations and realize that with diligence, judgment, work, and a bit of luck, a house like one of these could be yours. There are plenty more houses to go — for a song, even one sung badly out of tune.

# YOU WILL ALSO WANT TO READ:

❏ **14185 HOW TO BUILD YOUR OWN LOG HOME FOR LESS THAN $15,000,** *by Robert L. Williams.* When Robert L. Williams' North Carolina home was destroyed by a tornado, he and his family taught themselves how to construct a log home, even though they were unfamiliar with chain-saw construction techniques. In this practical, money-saving book, he clearly explains every step of the process. By following Williams' simple procedures, you can save tens, even hundreds of thousands of dollars, while building the rustic house you've always dreamed of owning. Profusely illustrated with diagrams and over 100 photographs, this is the best log-home construction book ever written. *1996, 8½ x 11, 224 pp, illustrated, soft cover.* $19.95.

❏ **14187 HOW TO LIVE WITHOUT ELECTRICITY — AND LIKE IT,** *by Anita Evangelista.* There's no need to remain dependent on commercial electrical systems for your home's comforts and security. This book describes many alternative methods that can help one become more self-reliant and free from the utility companies. Learn how to light, heat and cool your home, obtain and store water, cook and refrigerate food, and fulfill many other household needs without paying the power company! Complete with numerous illustrations and photographs, as well as listings for the best mail-order sources for the products depicted, this is a complete sourcebook for those who wish to both simplify and improve their lives. *1997, 5½ x 8½, 168 pp, illustrated, soft cover.* $13.95.

❏ **17054 HOW TO BUY LAND CHEAP, Fifth Edition,** *by Edward Preston.* This is the bible of bargain-basement land buying. the author bought 8 lots for a total sum of $25. He shows you how to buy good land all over the country for not much more. This book has been revised, with updated addresses and new addresses added. This book will take you through the process for finding cheap land, evaluating and bidding on it, and closing the deal. Sample form letters are also included to help you get started and get results. You can buy land for less than the cost of a night out — this book shows how. *1996, 5½ x 8½, 136 pp, illustrated, soft cover.* $14.95.

❏ **14176 HOW TO DEVELOP A LOW-COST FAMILY FOOD-STORAGE-SYSTEM,** *by Anita Evangelista.* If you're weary of spending a large percentage of your income on your family's food needs, they you should follow this amazing book's numerous tips on food-storage techniques. Slash your food bill by over fifty percent, and increase your self-sufficiency at the same time through alternative ways of obtaining, processing and storing foodstuffs. Includes methods of freezing, canning, drying, brandying, and many other food-preservation procedures. *1995, 5½ x 8½, 120 pp, illustrated, soft cover.* $10.00.

❏ **14175 SELF-SUFFICIENCY GARDENING, Financial, Physical and Emotional Security from Your Own Backyard,** *by Martin P. Waterman.* A practical guide of organic gardening techniques that will enable anyone to grow vegetables, fruits, nuts, herbs, medicines and other useful products, thereby increasing self-sufficiency and enhancing the quality of life. Includes sections of edible landscaping, greenhouses, hydroponics and computer gardening (including the Internet), seed saving and propagation, preserving and storing crops, and much more including fact filled appendices. *1995, 8½ x 11, 128 pp, illustrated, indexed, soft cover.* $13.95.

*And much, much more.* **We offer the very finest in controversial and unusual books — a complete catalog is sent** *FREE* **with every book order. If you would like to order the catalog separately, please see our ad on the next page.**

● ● ● ● ● ● ● ● ● ● ● ● ● ● ● ● ● ● ● ● ● ● ● ● ● ● ● ● ●

HM97

**LOOMPANICS UNLIMITED**
**PO BOX 1197**
**PORT TOWNSEND, WA 98368**

Please send me the books I have checked above. I am enclosing $ _____ (which includes $4.95 for the shipping and handling of books totaling $20. Please include $1 for each additional $20 ordered. *Washington residents please include 7.9% for sales tax.*

NAME _____

ADDRESS _____

CITY/STATE/ZIP _____

We accept Visa and MasterCard. To place a credit card order *only,*
call 1-800-380-2230, Monday through Friday, 8am to 4pm, PST.